Aboriginal Education in Canada:
A Plea for Integration

John W. Friesen, Ph.D.
Virginia Lyons Friesen, Ph.D.

Detselig Enterprises, Ltd.

Calgary, Alberta

Canadian Cataloguing in Publication Data
Friesen, John W
  Aboriginal education

  Includes bibliographical references.
  ISBN 1-55059-241-6
  1. Indians of North America – Education – Canada. I. Friesen,
  Virginia Agnes Lyons, II. Title
  E96.2F74 2002 371.829'97071 C2002-910793-8

Detselig Enterprises Ltd.
210, 1220 Kensington Road NW
Calgary, Alberta T2N 3P5

Phone: (403) 283-0900
Fax: (403) 283-6947
email: temeron@telusplanet.net
www.temerondetselig.com

We acknowledge the financial support of the Government of Canada
through the Book Industry Development Program (BPIDP) for our
publishing program.

Printed in Canada   SAN 115-0324   ISBN 1-55059-241-6

To our friends,

Mark and Kim Lan,

two excellent conversationalists.

Contents

Preface ix
A Note on Terminology x
Acknowledgements xi

1   The Need for Integrated Education 13
     Historical Happenings 14
     Positive Update 16
     The Ecological Appeal 18
     The Spiritual Appeal 19
     The Appeal for Humanity 19
     Reality Check 22

2   Profiling Canadian Aboriginal Education 25
     Prevailing Educational Frontiers 26
        The Teaching Milieu 26
        Language Maintenance 29
        Acknowledging Learning Styles 31
        Culturally-Relevant Curriculum 33
        Incorporating Indigenous Knowledge 35

3   Traditional Aboriginal Philosophy 39
     Aboriginal Origins 41
     Tribal World-View 44
        A Holistic Global Perspective 45
        An Appreciation for Life and Family 50
        A Caring and Sharing Society 53
        A Spiritual Sense of Community 57
     Conclusion 59

4   Traditional Aboriginal Pedagogy 63
     Defining the Oral Tradition 64
        Dimensions of the Oral Tradition 65
        Structure of the Oral Tradition 67
        Emergence of Written Forms 68

The Utility of Legends 68
Legend Typology 69
Parameters of Legend Telling 74
Legend Supplements 75
The Implications of Process 76

5   The Evolution of Aboriginal Education in Canada 81
Canadian Explorations 81
East Coast Campaign 82
Western Campaign 84
The Persistence of Indian Educational Policy 87
Twentieth Century Developments 88
White Paper, Red Paper 90
National Indian Brotherhood Response 92
Assembly of First Nations Response 93
The Royal Commission on Aboriginal Affairs 95
Education Proposals 97
Standing Senate Committee on Aboriginal Peoples Response . .97

6   The Residential School Phenomenon 99
Origins of the System 101
Pre-Confederation Practices 102
Post-Confederation Policy 104
Twentieth Century Developments 107
Life in Residential Schools 109
Daily Schedules 110
School Content 112
The Aftermath 114
Residential School Litigations 115
Student Memories 116

7   Métis Education in Canada 119
Towards Formal School Systems 123
Saskatchewan 123
Alberta 124
Manitoba 125
Problems and Complexities 127
MacNeil Commission 129
Camperville, Manitoba 131
Analysis 131

8   The Twenty-First Century Frontier 137
Continuing Frontiers 138
Aboriginal Self-Government 138
Land Claims 139
Residential School Litigations 140
Urban Transitions 140
Indian Act Revisions 141
Future Directions for Aboriginal Schooling 143
The Final Charge 145

References 149

Index 165

Book Cover by David J Friesen and Alvin Choong

The eagle is viewed as a special bird by North American First Nations. The eagle takes great pride in the strength of his wings and represents power and wisdom.

Preface

For thousands of years the Stoney people gained an education from the tribal elders which fitted them to live with pride and confidence on this Great Island . . . a sound education in the three Rs has become essential for survival. In my father's time this was not so. . . .Today in schooling we need the best available – plus . . . we [must] integrate the wisdom of our culture with the knowledge of the technology of the other culture – *Chief John Snow,* 1977: 153-156.

A few decades ago the Indigenous People of Canada were at an educational crossroads; should they try to maintain their traditional way of life or give in to the pressures of assimilation? It now appears they have made their decision. They will not retreat to the past, neither will they blindly fold into the structures of dominant society. Instead, as Chief John Snow has suggested, they will maintain their traditional cultural distinctives and integrate into their worldview what they deem to be useful from "the other culture." The process through which this fusion will hopefully come about is education.

To appreciate the immense agony and soul-searching this resolution has required, it is necessary to trace the evolutionary path of Indigenous education from before first contact to the 21st century. Several chapters of this book purport to do that, preceded by a unique challenge to Native people themselves. First Nations have an immensely formidable selling job to do, to convince the Canadian nonNative public that unless we regain a deep respect for planet Earth there is no future for the human race. This, and other presuppositions about the universe, are deeply imbedded in Indigenous knowledge which desperately needs to be integrated into the information highway of the public domain. We call on Indigenous elders to initiate a campaign of sharing their insights with a needy human race. This imposing challenge may require a slight shuffling of agenda, substituting a commitment to survival for more political goals. As the Native community is well aware, an integration of Indigenous knowledge could provide an element of certainty to the future.

A Note on Terminology

We live in a day when the political correctness syndrome has virtually dominated the national scene and challenged every attempt at meaningful communication. It is therefore quite difficult to delineate or define relevant terms to everyone's satisfaction. Against this background, this risk will still be taken here in the interest of trying to maintain some semblance of communication.

Naturally, there are a variety of terms to choose from in writing about the original occupants of this continent. One can choose from Aboriginal Peoples, AmerIndians, First Nations, First Peoples, Indians, Indigenous Peoples, Native Peoples, and North American Indians. Recently Anita Friesen, a retired teacher at Loon Lake, SK, was informed that the First Peoples be called "PreCanadians!"

There are writers, Native and nonNative, who prefer a particular usage to the exclusion of all the others. Currently the Government of the United States and writers in that country seem to prefer the term "Indian," while Canadians are opting for "First Nations, Indigenous People, or Aboriginals." Despite arguments to the contrary, a variety of these descriptions will be employed in the ensuing pages, partially to relieve monotony in delivery, and partly because it is difficult to know which usage might be appropriate in any given context. In addition, words to describe the First Peoples will be capitalized as a means of emphasizing the literary legitimacy of writing about the AmerIndians, in the same way that identities of other nationalities are capitalized.

Acknowledgements

Over recent years we have been fortunate in being able to visit many First Nations communities in every state between Alberta and Arizona and Texas, as well as Canada's five westerly provinces. The University of Calgary's Native Outreach Program has enabled us to experience many other teaching/learning opportunities involving students from early childhood to college age. Many members of the Stoney First Nation have served as our private tutors from 1988 to 2001 when we were involved there on a formal basis. These individuals deserve a very warm thank you for their patient and caring instruction.

We would like to acknowledge the assistance of Dr. Ted Giles, May Misfeldt, and Linda Berry of Detselig/Temeron Publishers for their dedicated efforts in making this work available. We also say thank you to our children, Bruce, Karen, Gaylene, David, and Beth Anne (and their spouses), and our grandchildren (all ten of them), for their patience in listening to our sometimes unsolicited lectures on "meaningful experiences in Aboriginal country." Their many visits to our place of work on the Stoney Indian Reserve were greatly appreciated. Thanks are also due our friend, Mark C. Y. Lan, who read the entire manuscript and offered many helpful suggestions.

Finally, we want to express our appreciation to the various First Nations for welcoming us into their communities through the years. If this book in any way motivates them to more enthusiastically share the richness of their cultural perspective with their fellow nonAboriginal Canadians, it will have been worth the effort of writing it.

J. W. F.

V. L. F.

Calgary, Alberta

John W. Friesen, Ph.D., D.Min., D.R.S., is a Professor in the Faculty of Education and the Faculty of Communication and Culture at the University of Calgary where he teaches courses in Aboriginal history and education. He is an ordained minister with the All Native Circle Conference of the United Church of Canada, and served as Minister of Morley United Church on the Stoney Indian Reserve from 1986 to 2001. He is the author of more than 30 books including:

People, Culture & Learning (Detselig, 1977);

Introduction to Teaching: A Socio-Cultural Approach (co-author), (Kendall/Hunt, 1990);

When Cultures Clash: Case Studies in Multiculturalism (Detselig, 1993);

You Can Get There From Here: The Mystique of North American Plains Indians Culture & Philosophy (Kendall/Hunt, 1995);

The Real/Riel Story: An Interpretive History of the Métis People of Canada (Borealis, 1996);

Rediscovering the First Nations of Canada (Detselig, 1997);

Sayings of the Elders: An Anthology of First Nations Wisdom (Detselig, 1998);

First Nations of the Plains: Creative, Adaptable and Enduring (Detselig, 1999); and,

Aboriginal Spirituality and Biblical Theology: Closer Than You Think, (Detselig, 2000).

Virginia Lyons Friesen, Ph.D., is a self-employed Early Childhood Education Consultant and holds a Certificate in Counseling from the Institute of Pastoral Counseling in Akron, Ohio. She has many years of teaching experience in early childhood education and has co-presented a number of papers at academic conferences.

She is co-editor of *Grade Expectations: A Multicultural Handbook for Teachers,* (Alberta Teachers Association, 1995), and co-author of *In Defense of Public Schools in North America* (Detselig, 2001). She served as Director of Christian Education with the Morley United Church on the Stoney Indian Reserve from 1988 to 2001.

One

The Need for Integrated Education

During the late 1960s when the phrase "integrated Indian education" was all the rage, John Snow, then Chief of the Wesley Band of the Stoney (Nakoda Sioux) First Nation, made the following statement: "Of course I believe in integrated education. Let the neighboring communities bring their children onto our reserve and we'll do our best to integrate them."

Most educators of that time, listening to Chief Snow, would probably have thought he could not be serious. After all, the reverse plan was the order of the day. It was 1969 and the federal government had recently announced its latest innovation regarding Indian policy. The plan was to remove Aboriginal children from federally-run reserve schools and integrate them with nonNative students in provincial schools. The underlying premise on which the new plan was based was clearly assimilation, not integration. This was emphatically borne out when the infamous federal White Paper of 1969 was published. At that point the federal government showed its true colors, having decided on a policy that would pave the way for Canada's First Nations to abandon their legal status and take up the lifestyle of all other Canadians. The government White Paper proposed that the Indian Act be abolished, the treaties be ignored, and the Department of Indian Affairs be eliminated. Aboriginal peoples were henceforth to receive all services such as health, education, and welfare through provincial channels.

Naturally the stunned Native community quickly reacted to these federal proposals. Indian leaders were particularly upset that they had not been consulted about the radical policy change before it was announced. A series of critical papers soon emerged out of the Aboriginal community forcing the government to backtrack and relegate the new plan to a backburner. The government-style educational integration plan, it seemed, was seriously out of step with the Native perspective.

Lest the concept of educational integration be permanently relegated to the historic past, however, there may be some advantage in examining the implications of a more culturally-relevant format. Perhaps Chief Snow was right; perhaps nonNative children ought to at least occasionally be immersed in the rudiments of Aboriginal culture so they could learn to appreciate it. The insights gleaned from the last few decades of cross-cultural research have underscored the fact that such measures could have great mutual benefit. To begin with, there are very few historical examples of cultures that have demonstrated the capability of survival and endurance that the Aboriginal peoples have. The stamina of the First Nations worldview has been validated by the fact that for centuries their way of life has been attacked, harassed, and victimized, but it has persisted. When the fur trade screeched to a halt, the Indigenous peoples suddenly became the white man's burden. Aboriginals were told that told that their way of life was gone forever, and their religious beliefs were in need of a makeover. For generations young Native children read in schoolbooks about the "savage ways" of their ancestors and governments banned the practice of sacred ceremonies like the sundance and the potlatch.

For a long while it seemed as though the cultural genocide of Canada's Indians was assured. Until the 1930s the population of North American Aboriginals was on a slide, and the "Indian problem" was apparently going to resolve itself without too much outside interference. Then things began to change as the First Nations gained a bit of resistance to imported diseases and adopted new diets. Soon their population began to stabilize and then grow. By the 1960s, some thirty years later, a rigorous program of cultural revitalization began as the Indigenous peoples gained physical numbers and spiritual strength. When the program to integrate their children in nonNative schools was initiated, Aboriginal parents began to express their concerns. In 1970 a sit-in at the Blue Quills School in St. Paul, in northeast Alberta, ushered in the first Aboriginal-controlled school in Canada.

Historical Happenings

The educational sufferings of the First Nations comprise an unfortunate chapter in Canada's history. Books documenting the experiences of those who survived the residential schools, for example, relate horrifying stories of physical abuse and suffering, hunger, and psychological stress (Haig-Brown, 1993; Knockwood, 1994; Furniss, 1995; Grant, 1996; Dyck, 1997; Miller, 1997; and Milloy, 1999). Today's courts are jammed with litigation claims against the federal government and the religious denominations that ran these schools. These sorrowful situations are complemented with federal calls to change the Indian Act, resolve land claims, and define Aboriginal self-government. It will take an extremely hardy culture to endure these complicated challenges and still survive, but the Indigenous peoples will be up to it. History has shown that they can endure these kinds of challenges and still retain their inner strength. The evidence is they will not only survive but thrive.

Based on the reality that Aboriginal culture may be characterized by adaptability, endurance, and creativity (Friesen, 1999) one cannot help but wonder what future forms it may take. To the modern way of thinking, the traditional Indian way of life was certainly simplistic, compared with the wondrous accomplishments of the computer chip age. It probably took centuries to invent tools with any noticeable characteristics of engineering sophistication. Today it is only a matter of days before the latest technological devices are thrown out with other refuse. Despite this reality, as well as having been victims of deliberate cultural genocide, Native cultures have survived. Before European contact, some Aboriginal tribes engaged in occasional migrations and geographic adaptations, sometimes induced by climatic conditions, other natural forces, or tribal conflicts, but their cultures persisted.

A deeper look at the philosophical foundations of the traditional Aboriginal lifestyle reveals that the underlying presuppositions of their worldview were spiritual. The First Peoples perceived spirits in everything, in both animate and inanimate objects, and in plants as well as in creatures of the sky, the ocean, and the earth. They respected these spirits and held great reverence for them. After all, in a world in which everything was viewed as being interconnected, everything and everyone depended on everything and everyone else for survival. The traditional belief was that if a warrior killed an animal for food he prayed and thanked the animal spirit for the means of sustenance provided for him. He might then return meat from the slaughtered animal to the earth in thanksgiving. The reality of interconnectedness necessitated that the warrior appreciate his role in the scheme of things and on occasion remind himself that he too might be called on to sacrifice for the greater good.

Before European contact, the ceremonies, rituals, and observances of the First Peoples were premised on spiritual principles. These beliefs originated through metaphysical avenues, such as visions, and they were enacted in an atmosphere of faith, reverence, and devotion. Formal religious organizations known as sodalities or secret societies, headed by shamans or elders, were entrusted with preserving and passing on knowledge pertaining to the sacred ceremonies by means of the oral tradition. The elders would teach the secrets to selected youth who could then do the same for the next generation. By this means sacred knowledge was protected though additions or reinterpretations of it were made from time to time as new revelations were received.

All seemed to go well until the Europeans came. Armed with superior weaponry and knowledge (at least they thought so), it took only a short time before many Indian tribes were wiped out or conquered by military might. Unlike the United States, Canada chose a less military approach and opted for a more legal route in settling with the First Nations. Following a tradition set by the French and British governments, beginning in 1871, the Canadian government negotiated ten major treaties with the Aboriginals. The treaties allegedly transferred the ownership of Indian lands to the newly-established national government and relegated the First Nations to small pieces of real estate (often unfertile plots of land) known as reserves, where it was perceived that they would eventually die out. The importation of infectious diseases and alcohol worked to the invaders' advantage as corollary factors in effecting the demise of the Aboriginals.

In addition to making arrangements regarding land ownership, Canada's Indian treaties made provisions regarding agricultural tools, cattle, and seed to establish the Indians as farmers. No government official seriously considered fulfilling the promises made in the treaties, and no one bothered to investigate what the Aboriginals understood by the process. After all, the Aboriginals were dying out. Years later it was suggested that negotiating Indian leaders thought they were signing peace treaties, not transferring ownership of lands. After all, no one really owned the land; it belonged to the Creator who had arranged for His people to benefit from its resources (Hildebrandt, Carter, and First Rider, 1996). As time went on many Aboriginals were lured to urban centres in search of employment and a better standard of living than was possible on reserves (Buckley, 1993). A survey of living conditions on reserves at that time indicate they were, and in many cases still are, devastating places to live. Negative statistics pertaining to lack of economic and educational opportunity, poor housing, inadequate health facilities, and social deprivation are still very high. Reports of high rates of alcoholism, family abuse, and suicide are regularly featured in daily newspapers.

Positive Update

Today a miracle is happening. The First Nations of Canada are again demonstrating that theirs is a culture of survival and endurance. Indian population growth is evident, and life expectancy has dramatically increased. As late as 1973, the average Native individual in Canada could expect to live to 43 years while the average Canadian (including Natives) could expect to live 62 years. By 1983 these figures were 43 years and 67 years respectively. By 1995 the figures rose so that Indian males could expect to live to be 69 compared with 75 years for Canadian males as whole. Indian women could expect to live to be 76 compared with 82 years for Canadian women as a whole (Frideres and Gadacz, 2001: 66-67).

The Indian miracle also includes other positive features. Today Aboriginal youth are staying in school longer and more of them are graduating from post-secondary institutions. The Indian cultural renaissance that began in the 1960s is gaining momentum. Celebrations of traditional ceremonies and rituals are increasing. Elders are beginning to share their spiritual secrets on a wider scale (Couture, 1991a) and intertribal sharing of knowledge is occurring. NonNatives are becoming interested in learning about Native ways and their curiosity is being accommodated by receptive elders. A recent exhibition of Blackfoot cultures at the Alberta Glenbow Museum in Calgary is a case in point. The exhibit took four years to develop and involved all four Blackfoot Nations – Kainai or Blood, Peigan, Siksika, and the Blackfeet Nation (Southern Peigan) of Montana. There have literally been thousands of visitors to the exhibit, eagerly examining displays, admiring paintings, watching informative videos, and asking questions of Native guides.

The economic picture for Canada's First Nations is brighter as band councils begin to involve themselves in negotiations with resource companies for local industrial development. Many bands are currently partnered with resource companies and manufacturing firms to build economically sustaining industries on site and provide employment for their increasing populations. Even the federal government is relinquishing their hold on decision-making regarding First Nations without first consulting with Indian leaders. No policy changes are being inaugurated without full consultation with all parties concerned from local band councils to National Indian organizations. Canada's First Nations are finally being heard.

So where does integration fit into this scenario? It fits in front and centre, and should be the primary goal of contemporary Aboriginal education today. The new emphasis is that educational integration must become a priority within the Aboriginal milieu. The new objective of integrating outsiders into Aboriginal ways of thinking and behaving must be undertaken by Aboriginal educators and leaders. This book is a plea to them to do this – for everyone's benefit and for the sake of the future. It is an appeal to the Aboriginal people of Canada to promote integration – the kind of which Chief John Snow spoke nearly forty years ago. NonNative peoples need to be integrated into Native ways because the ancient sacred ways have so much to offer. This task can only be undertaken by Native peoples because they alone possess the needed knowledge. The appeal has three urgent components – ecological, spiritual, and humane.

The Ecological Appeal

One of the most neglected, albeit intelligent prophets of our time, is scientist David Suzuki, who has been reminding Canadians for decades that the earth, on whose resources we rely for our very existence, has been seriously violated. Suzuki laments that modern humankind has conveniently distanced itself from the natural world and lost what the First Peoples once had as a foundation of their lives. Today people are increasingly surrounded by and becoming dependent upon the inventions of the scientific world and neglecting the forces that sustain them. By losing a meaningful and appreciative worldview, that nature is the sustainer of us all, people have become devoted to consumerism and lost their connection to the natural world (Suzuki, 1997: 25).

Suzuki points with hope to the vast repositories of essential knowledge that still exist in traditional societies. Ignoring this, modern science has obviously developed an inadequate worldview that has proven incapable of recognizing the delicate balance between natural and spiritual commodities. Suzuki calls for a greater respect on the part of scientists for the wisdom inherent in traditional societies. This wisdom has always reflected respect for the earth and all life upon it. As Battiste (2000a: 201-202) notes:

> . . . immigrant society is sorely in need of what Aboriginal knowledge has to offer. We are witnessing throughout the world the weaknesses in knowledge based on science and technology. It is costing us our air, our water, our earth; our very lives are at stake. No longer are we able to turn to science to rid us of the mistakes of the past or to clean up our planet for the future of our children.

Lest this discussion suggest that all scientists ignore these warnings and therefore should be tarred with the same tainted brush, it is appropriate to note a statement issued by the Union of Concerned Scientists and quoted by Suzuki (1997: 27):

> As scientists, many of us have profound experiences of awe and reverence before the universe. We understand that what is regarded as sacred is more likely to be treated with care and respect. Our planetary home should be so regarded. Efforts to safeguard and cherish the environment need to be infused with a vision of the sacred.

Concerned statements notwithstanding, if Suzuki is correct, the universe is still in deep trouble and our current enamor with consumerism will not alleviate it. Obviously something will have to be done before long and there is evidence that the call to study the traditional ecological orientations of First Nations is urgent (Battiste and Henderson, 2000).

The Spiritual Appeal

A Blackfoot (Siksika) informant once suggested that a favored tribal way of teaching a ritual, ceremony, or other revered practice was in four steps. *First*, initiates would verbally be informed about the ritual or sacred practice; *second,* they would be invited to observe it; *third*, they would be invited to participate in it; and, after sufficient such experience would; *fourth,* be permitted and authorized to teach it to others. By continual enactment of the revered practice, the essence of the practiced ceremony would more indelibly be stamped in the individual's mind and heart.

The Siksika teaching method makes good sense and should perhaps should be taken up by national Indian leaders and knowledgeable elders in relation to the education of nonNatives. The first step appears to be getting underway in that nonAboriginals have available a multiplicity of sources by which to learn about Indigenous ways. Informative books and other publications, written by both Native and nonNative writers have filtered down from libraries and bookstores to school classrooms and private homes. Evidence that the second step is underway includes the fact that increasing numbers of nonNatives have become frequent guests at such events as pow-wows, rodeos, and by invitation at some sacred ceremonial rituals. On occasion First Nations leaders have invited nonNative guests to observe (second step) and even participate in (third step) pipe, sweetgrass, and sweat-lodge ceremonies, and more rarely in the sundance. Now it is time to strengthen the third stage by launching invitational campaigns to teach the old ways to those who want to learn.

The virtue of "evangelizing" the uninformed with the Indigenous gospel of tradition is twofold. *First,* such knowledge can greatly alleviate some of the mistrust and apprehension that nonNative Canadians have towards Indian ways. Being properly informed fosters understanding, and goodwill and provides a solid framework for negotiating about other matters. *Second,* the very act of instructing tends to reinforce the importance of subject matter for those engaged in the act of teaching. If there is any fear about losing Indigenous knowledge in the form of valued beliefs and practices, there is no better way to assure its perpetuity than by engaging in it as a medium of instruction. The fulfilment of such an objective can in no way demean the spiritual essence of the practice; it will only serve to reinforce its value in that it has been thought sufficiently worthy of perpetuation.

There is another benefit to be derived from a rigorous program of Aboriginal integration and it is this. There is mounting evidence that many Indian youth are losing their sense of reverence for the old ways. Increasingly they are becoming attached to the world of fast cars, video machines, computer games, and capitalism generally. Many Aboriginal languages are fast disappearing as English and French media continue to provide entertainment and other thought forms for all of the nation's youth. Indigenous young people are no exception in this regard. They are buying into the same forms of cultural engagement as their nonNative peers. They are no longer speaking their traditional languages. Indian leaders are bemoaning this reality and begging the federal government to do something about it. It is of the utmost importance to remember that government-funded language programs are of little value in assuring language maintenance. The fact is that eight of Canada's ten provinces have adopted policies regarding the maintenance of Aboriginal languages, but only those in the Yukon and the Northwest Territories have proven to have much merit. As Quebec's National Assembly stated, "Aboriginal nations are primarily responsible for safeguarding and developing their languages" (Fettes and Norton, 2000: 38).

The cold fact about language learning is that unless a language is spoken daily in the course of family activities, it has no real significance for the speaker. As Paupanekis and Westfall (2001: 89) state, "The prerequisite for keeping a language alive lies not in the schools, but in the home." The press for conformity crosses all cultural lines, including language. It includes the world of work, religion, leisure, education, and entertainment. Every female preteener and teenager in Canada, Native or nonNative, knows who Britney Spears is, and they all want to be just like her. Spears is American and she speaks only English.

By engaging in a compelling campaign to integrate nonNatives into the realm of Indigenous knowledge, its essence can be maintained and perpetuated in both communities – Aboriginal and nonAboriginal. This is a serious call to Native leaders to begin the campaign. Your students are waiting. In a sense this slogan has a great deal of merit; "By informing others, you may save yourselves."

The Appeal for Humanity

Porterfield (1990) suggests that AmerIndian spirituality may be viewed as a countercultural movement, but we believe the time has come to place Indian spirituality at the forefront of contemporary thinking. It is time to move to the next phase and instead of examining Indigenous knowledge as a philosophical curiosity, integrate its essence into mainstream knowledge. The counterculture metaphor implies an anti-stance, and as long as it remains only a considered position, Indigenous knowledge will not be appreciated for the insights it can rightly bring to the table. The strength and vitality is there, and there is no doubt that Aboriginal philosophers can hold their own right along with other metaphysical postulators who offer explanations about the workings of the universe.

The onus for integrating Indigenous knowledge must necessarily be placed on the shoulders of knowledgeable Native leaders. This may not sound fair or reasonable, but there can be no other approach. The rationale for this mandate is that Native elders alone have the knowledge to set things right. They will not necessarily be approached by nonNatives to share their insights, however, because the process has been reversed for too long. For the past several centuries, NonNative society has been in charge of teaching First Nations how to live, but there is increasing evidence that its teachers have run out of steam (Hanohano, 1999). Today the world is looking for answers to complex problems such as the one implicit in this question; "How can we maintain our increasing reliance on technology and stop damaging the universe?" The answer to that question, of course, is that priorities must change. Valuing the universe and its operations must be put on the highest rung of the ladder and excessive consumerism on the lowest one. Naturally this will require a different kind of lifestyle for the twenty-first century, but it could be a richer, fuller, more meaningful lifestyle. As the biblical Gospel of Luke (12:15 NIV) suggests, "A man's life does not consist in the abundance of his possessions." Of course most North Americans would probably agree with St. Luke's statement, and a few may even try to follow it. Before the European conquest, however, Aboriginal peoples lived by it.

By concentrating on a mission of integration, First Nations could shift their energies, at least partially, from negotiating with the federal government on such matters as treaties, the Indian Act, residential school litigations, Aboriginal self-government, and land claims. All of these are certainly legitimate pursuits, but they tend to cast First Nations in a negative light. Indians always appear to be hard done by. They consistently appear to be in a demanding mode, always asking for something, always making claims, always blaming someone for their misfortunes. The adversarial process of Indian versus government and society has gone on for decades and the media has made the most of it. After all, negative stories sell papers. Sadly, most Canadians believe what they encounter in the media. Rarely do they read about the positive aspects of Aboriginal culture because such themes are reserved only for community-produced television programs which few nonNatives Canadians watch. Do very many people really want to read about Indigenous spirituality, ecological respect, tribal customs, religious rituals, sharing, healing, and meditation?

Stated positively, Indigenous cultures have knowledge to offer by which to enrich our thinking. By engaging in an aggressive, yet reasonable campaign to acquaint their nonNative counterparts with the essence of

Aboriginal philosophy, First Nations will undoubtedly gain a great deal more public acceptance than they have in the last few decades. Indulging in blaming, name-calling, and launching negative campaigns will win no respect, least of all those who hold the power to amend the very institutional structures which can assist Native peoples in accessing their full rights. Battiste and Henderson (2000: 21), for example, blame Eurocentric thinking for all Aboriginal ills:

> As a theory it [Eurocentric thought] postulates the superiority of Europeans over non-Europeans. It is built on a set of assumptions and beliefs that educated and unusually unprejudiced Europeans and North Americans habitually accept as true, as supported by "the facts," or as "reality."

Battiste and Henderson go on to suggest that Eurocentric thought results in a single world centre, namely Europe, and its surrounding periphery. According to these authors, North Americans have apparently never been able to release themselves from the grasp of European thought, despite the formulation of the American Declaration of Independence in 1776 or the founding of Canada as an independent nation in 1867.

Obviously there must be room for this kind of debate, at least in academic circles, and there is certainly truth in Battiste and Henderson's postulations. Unfortunately, politicians and the body politick have little patience for this kind of diatribe and they will likely brush it aside. Sadly, too much of polemics can quickly erode meaningful dialogue and both parties will soon be back where they started from. Positive integrative programs launched by Aboriginal leaders could build meaningful bridges of understanding between Natives and nonNatives in North America. With understanding as a foundation it will be possible to develop concern and compassion for one another's needs and interests and together forge solutions to problematic situations.

Reality Check

There is an additional matter that should be raised in this context, although the nature of it is rather delicate. Aboriginal leaders are fond of bandying about the word colonization when referring to the dissolution of their rights by national government (Adams, 1999; Battiste, 2000; Binda and Calliou, 2001). It may sound harsh to suggest it, but the subject brings up an unfortunate phenomenon in Native communities, namely the colonization of Aboriginal peoples by their own leaders (Adams, 1999; Flanagan, 2000). Although overburdened by their altercations with government, this arena presents another formidable Indian foe. It constitutes a corollary agenda for Canada's First Nations to pursue if they want to bring a measure of authenticity to the bargaining table. The phenomenon of intracolonization is a sad reality, a blight on many Indigenous communities. The fact that it goes on in Canada can only hamper the legality of Indian claims.

An outspoken opponent of Aboriginal rights is Thomas Flanagan, a University of Calgary political scientist. Flanagan is in consensus with the late Howard Adams that the contemporary status of neocolonialism in Indian communities encourages upper echelon Natives to adopt conservative middle class ideologies and superimpose them on their unsuspecting peers (Flanagan, 2000). These leaders colonize their own people in the same manner that they claim to have been colonized. Adams claimed that universities which house Native studies departments foster neocolonialism by educating the Native elite to fill the role abandoned by government bureaucrats. As he put it:

> In short, it involves giving some benefits of the dominant society to a small, privileged minority of Aboriginals in return for their help in pacifying the majority. This use of an educated Native elite to help governments deal with the 'Native problem' has its parallels around the world. (Adams, 1999: 54)

Flanagan documents a series of flagrant violations of tribal trust by untrustworthy Aboriginal leaders, pointing out the exceedingly high salaries which some elected Indian leaders pay themselves, their indulgence in nepotism after they are elected, and their squandering of band funds. While this kind of financial rampage goes on, negative social indicators such as suicide, violent crimes, high accident rate, and substance abuse continue to flourish. In 1998 the Department of Indian Affairs estimated that it would have to intervene with "remedial management plans" in the case of 20 to 25 percent of Indian bands (Flanagan, 2000: 90-92).

Cross (2001: 11), an Aboriginal volunteer with a Mennonite Native Ministries organization in Saskatoon, states;

> A hierarchy of exploitation is in place in North American aboriginal communities. In each community a handful of male tribal chiefs, presidents and their executives place heavy burdens on their people. This means women are oppressed, children neglected and communities held in poverty. The tribal executive favors voters who keep them in power. The tribal leaders have the power to take community funds in the form of lucrative salaries and expense accounts, creating a small but powerful elite. Billions of dollars flow into tribal government while welfare roles increase.

Boldt (1993: 141) echoes a similar sentiment when he observes that blind faith is often placed in Native leaders for economic development or for the resolution of problematic situations with unfortunate results. Often the biological appearances of elected Indian bureaucrats (Native faces instead of nonNative faces) are the only things that change when forms of Aboriginal self-government replace government imperialism. Newly-selected First Nations bureaucrats may attempt to justify their actions by suggesting that "they learned the art of corruption from their nonNative counterparts," but, hopefully, this unwarranted form of self-justification will satisfy no one for very long. Jull (1992) points out that in traditional times Native leaders were humble people who were close to their people, they served rather than bossed, and they kept their people informed. Perhaps it is time that Aboriginal leaders began to practice traditional Native Indian ways.

In analyzing Aboriginal colonization, these questions must be raised, "What happened to the efficacy of Indigenous thought? How can community-selected leaders so brazenly ignore the teachings of their elders? Must Eurocentric colonizing tendencies, which have obviously influenced their thinking, always prevail over traditional common sense? Can we at this point expect these individuals to take responsibility for their actions and show genuine concern for their people?" Some wealthy Indian bands, for example, have chosen not to use any of their own resources for preventative social programs such as family care or alleviation of substance abuse. Instead they wantonly waste their resources while railing on government for additional monies to counteract obvious increases in devastating habits. When will these Aboriginal leaders begin to take responsibility for their own people?

Until these questions are answered by the Native people themselves there is little reason to believe that many nonNatives will rally to the Aboriginal cause. It may be Eurocentric to suggest it, but unless the Indigenous people begin to clean up their own houses instead of demanding that others do it for them, few people will be convinced of their sincerity. Even fewer will engage in activities to aid their cause. This may not be an ideal state of affairs, nor even a particularly desirable situation, but it is reality. That reality may be labelled Eurocentric, but labelling will change nothing. As Andrea Bear Nicholas (2001: 29) states, ". . . it is the Native Peoples themselves who hold the key to their own liberation."

Two

Profiling Canadian Aboriginal Education

The educational and socialization processes of the various First Nations cultures throughout this country were seriously undermined by the formal education system that imposed upon the people some very different values and denigrated their spiritual practices, their languages, and their overall way of life.... First Nations cultures must once again be respected and the traditional values must again be held in high esteem. (Kirkness and Bowman, 1983: 103)

While more than one million Canadians can lay claim to Native ancestry, the official legal count of Status Indians is less than 700 000. This number is subject to rapid change, however, due to the high birth rate among Indigenous peoples (nearly 3 percent annually), and the fact that since 1985, via the passing of Bill C-31, those who previously lost Status through various means could apply to regain it. More than 90 000 individuals have regained Status since 1985.

About one-fourth of Canada's Aboriginal people live in Ontario while Saskatchewan and British Columbia are each host to another 16 percent. Nearly two-thirds of Status Indians (58%) live on reserves, while the rest (42%) live in cities and towns. There are more than 2 000 reserves in Canada, with over 600 residential bands. Most bands consist of about 500 members with only 11 bands in Canada consisting of a population of over 2 000. Most of these are located in Ontario and Alberta. The largest reserve in Canada is the Blood (Kainai) Nation in southern Alberta, while the most populated reserve is Six Nations at Brantford, Ontario.

Living conditions on most Indian reserves are less than desirable. The infant mortality rate is double that of the rest of the nation (17.5 per 1000 births versus 7.9 per 1000 births), poverty, unemployment, inadequate housing, and poor health conditions are a harsh reality, and educational attainment is low. Although positive changes are slowly being made, the major challenge is accessibility to adequate services which is both difficult and costly (Frideres and Gadacz, 2001: 78). Coupled with these realities is the fact that many Native people are migrating to urban areas where they are having to contend with a myriad of other challenges such as cultural alienation, racism, and economic deprivation (Buckley, 1993; Fox and Long, 2000).

Canadian First Nations were not able to participate fully in the Canadian economy during the 20th century. During the middle of the century when the country's economy moved from an agricultural base to one of technology, the Indian economy lagged behind, many times restricted by law from engaging in economic development. In some cases Aboriginals were refused licences to act as commercial big game hunting outfitters in areas where nonNatives had established ventures. They were also forbidden to take homestead lands which were reserved for incoming nonNative settlers. Finally, when the Canadian northlands opened up inland commercial fisheries, Natives were restricted from competing with nonNatives (Frideres, 1993: 464). Against this background it has been very difficult for First Nations people to make satisfactory adjustments to changing economic conditions.

Prevailing Educational Frontiers

The educational scene regarding First Nations in Canada is a bit more optimistic. As band councils continue to take over local schools there is a tendency for school programs to reflect local cultural customs and values. This means that Native children are experiencing increased opportunities to learn about their heritage. Adjustments required as this trend continues, however, incorporate a number of complex frontiers. These include: obtaining the services of culturally knowledgable and culturally sensitive teachers; incorporating language learning into school curricula; acknowledging and teaching towards traditional Aboriginal learning styles; developing locally-relevant curriculum materials; and, incorporating Indigenous knowledge into the curriculum, preferably by enhancing the role of elders in the classroom. It is hoped that the successful conquering of these frontiers will result in significantly reducing both school absenteeism and dropout rate in many Native communities.

The Teaching Milieu

One of the key recommendations of the Hawthorn Report of 1967 was that teachers should be encouraged to learn as much as possible about the background and culture of their First Nations students and take the initiative in getting to know individual students. This recommendation has perpetually been reiterated during the past three decades and is still a necessary emphasis (Wolcott, 1967; Friesen, 1977; Friesen, 1985; Elofson and Elofson, 1988; Reyhner, 1992; Duquette, 2000). This is because the majority of teachers in Aboriginal communities are still nonNative, and in many cases their knowledge of Native culture is quite limited. Taylor (1995) estimates that 90 percent of Native children will, at one time or another, be taught by a nonNative teacher.

Although many well-meaning and successful nonNative individuals have been effective teachers in Aboriginal communities, a number of recurring nonproductive practices which some teachers have engaged in must be noted. The primary concern has to do with motivation for some teachers taking jobs in Native communities because they cannot obtain a position elsewhere (Friesen, 1987a). As the school year gets underway teachers new to the vicissitudes of the northern frontier sometimes believe that if they can survive this kind of experience, they can survive anything. Unprepared for what they will encounter in a unique cultural milieu, the cultural gap simply overwhelms them and they fall prey to severe culture shock. The usual reaction is to shrink into a cocoon, function ineffectively, or simply resign and leave the community. The cocoon phenomenon occurs when nonNative teachers ignore the community and only interact with one another. By doing this they effectively form a private subculture in the community and are viewed as such. Some of their members may even entertain the perspective that since they are only temporarily in the community anyway, why bother to become a part of it?

A unique and useful concept emphasized by Taylor (1995) is the notion of low-context and high-context cultures. Taylor points out that Aboriginal cultures are generally high-context cultures in that the culture relies less on the spoken word and more on the context of existing, non-verbal information. Much is left unsaid in such cultural contexts because "everybody knows what everybody else is thinking." Conversely, EuroCanadian culture is low-context and relies a great deal on verbal interaction, body language, and gestures. NonNative teachers often experience frustration when they find that their students "simply won't open up." Similarly, they find that their Native colleagues will offer little help by way of explanation for puzzling events, customs, or happenings. The obvious solution to this dilemma is for nonNative teachers to form a working relationship with a community informant and be willing to learn from this liaison. Naturally, the extent to which learning can occur will depend on the sincerity of the nonNative teacher and the degree to which the two trust one another.

The element of trust will also be significant in terms of teacher-student relationships. Many Aboriginal students are quite used to being taught by a rotating teaching staff, that is, they may have to work with several teachers in the course of a year. Fortunately, this phenomenon is on a decline, partly because jobs are more scarce than they were a few decades ago, and partly because nonNative teachers are entering the arena of Native education better prepared. Regardless of the situation, the bottom line is that any student who reaches out to a teacher should never be denied.

Today many Indian bands are developing supplemental or substitute curricula for their schools through curriculum committees with the hope that Indigenous students will have greater opportunity to learn about their heritage. This is a positive development, but it poses a special challenge to nonNative teachers who may be unfamiliar with Aboriginal culture. In some respects it may also offer these teachers a second opportunity to learn about Native ways. The new curriculum may also supplement what the teachers have studied in their teacher training programs. Native-originated curricula may serve to reduce the cultural gap for First Nations students between school and community. It may help them feel more comfortable in school and possibly reduce the tension that may occur when the two cultures of nonNative and Native (teacher and student) meet.

The effectiveness with which teachers function has strong implications for teacher education programs delivered by universities and colleges. Several decades ago, a number of universities experimented with off-campus teacher education programs which were conducted on Indian reserves. This meant that university instructors and professors travelled to Native communities and taught accredited courses or conducted workshops on-site. Many of these programs were very successful. For the most part First Nations postsecondary students no longer had to leave their communities to obtain university education, until their last year of study. Before long, many Aboriginal individuals became qualified teachers in their home community schools (Friesen, 1991a; Grant, 1996).

Off-campus teacher education programs were not without unique benefits and challenges. One of the most obvious benefits was for university personnel to learn first-hand about Native community life. As regular visitors they soon became aware of aspects of local functioning which they could not learn about through textbook reading. Native students, on the other hand, particularly older students with family responsibilities, enjoyed the opportunity to study near home. A unique challenge implicit in the program was finding out how to make the program relevant to local needs and interests. Most university instructors who participated in the first off-campus teacher education programs were not acquainted with Indigenous ways, and they tended to function much in the way they did on campus. Few attempts were made to relate course content to local history or culture and the first university graduates from these programs usually received a typical nonNative-oriented kind of education. They were essentially being assimilated into a EuroCanadian way of thinking. This changed as instructors "learned on the job," and attempted to adapt the objectives of the subject matter they were teaching to a more relevant slant. Grant (1996) stresses the need for instructors in such situations to become culturally sensitive, nonjudgmental, and open to personal learning and growth. Hampton is less optimistic and charges that "Most, if not all, university education in Canada today is education for assimilation" (Hampton, 2000: 210).

A number of university off-campus programs are still in operation in First Nations communities today, although their emphasis has shifted from strictly concentrating on teacher education. Students who enroll in these programs are now able to pursue degrees in a variety of fields. The number of graduates from these programs has steadily risen, providing proof of the efficacy of this approach. Despite this success, the need for additional on campus course offerings in First Nations history, language, and culture still exists.

Language Maintenance

Social scientists have known for a long time that language is a conveyance of cultural content. The language of a culture incorporates all aspects of the respective cultural configuration including social, cognitive, linguistic, material, and spiritual elements. Leavitt (1995) notes that the most significant aspect of language is found in its ways of conceptualizing, preserving, and transmitting knowledge. Native languages, for example, tend to exemplify awareness of happenings, eventuating, change, flow, and interrelationships. This is because of a dominance of verbs. If these linguistic characteristics are to be appreciated, those languages must be kept alive. When a language disappears its implicit ways of conceptualization vanish.

Calliou (2001: 10) estimates that at least fifty of the fifty-three languages indigenous to Canada will disappear in the next century. In order to reduce this trend, many schools have designed Native language classes. Paupanekis and Westfall (2002: 101) warn that schools cannot rejuvenate Native languages, and when such programs are introduced, it is mandatory that Aboriginal parents be supportive. They will need to realize how an adequate Native language program will add to a child's total learning process. Sadly, there have been a few cases where parents have requested that their children be removed from Native language classes with no reason provided.

It is no secret that the foisting of English and French languages on the Indigenous community has been culturally costly. Indigenous myths and legends, for example, are seldom told in English or French, but when they are, the lessons they contain are not as clear as they might be if told in an Aboriginal language. When revered customs, rituals, and ceremonies are translated into foreign languages, their essence is often diminished or takes on new meaning. This development affects the social life of a culture as well. As new words, new meanings, and new emphases enter the domain of daily discourse, the very *geist* (spirit) of a culture can also change. If this trend is not satisfactory to those who stand to lose by it, it will be up to those who most value a given language to use any and all means at their disposal to preserve it.

All is not lost. Cultures can survive even if their members adopt a new language. This reality is that such an occurrence is part of the normal process of cultural change. Indigenous cultures, probably more than any other in the world, have demonstrated that they can make far-reaching cultural changes and still survive. Their history underscores this fact. The migrations of many First Nations across the North American continent before first contact, and their subsequent shifts in economy have proven this. Centuries ago many eastern Woodlands people migrated west and traded their agricultural economies for dependence on the buffalo. The moundbuilders of the southeast migrated to the northwest and their means of livelihood changed dramatically. Their language also changed to incorporate new realities. Still, despite these changes, they retained the spiritual rudiments of their culture.

Undoubtedly, the bent of this discussion will not please those Indigenous people who cling tenaciously to the idea that if their traditional language is replaced with another form, their culture will die out. The truth is that it will not likely die out, but it will change – probably to meet the times. This has happened in the past when the economies of Aboriginal cultures changed and it will likely happen again. Not all cultural changes in Indian country can be blamed on the infusion of European ideas. Many tribes significantly altered their lifestyle, long before first contact, due to such factors as intertribal wars, geographic shifts, migrations, new spiritual insights, and climactic changes.

Many cultural groups other than Aboriginals have experienced the necessity to alter or change languages. Dozens of national groups who immigrated to Canada over the past century have virtually abandoned their heritage languages and adopted French or English as their primary means of communication. Still, they treasure the values of their homeland and continue to practice significant elements of their heritage lifestyle. Canada, as a multicultural country not only permits this, but encourages it. The bottom line is that the responsibility for cultural maintenance appears to be in the hands of each cultural group. Speakers of a particular language (and some linguists and anthropologists) are the only ones who value it sufficiently enough to maintain it. Even if Aboriginal groups obtain governmental support and funding for extensive Indian language programs, there is no assurance they will be effective. Too many Aboriginal youth today prefer to speak English or French. They daily subject themselves to all manners of media influence, the bulk of which are transmitted in either of the country's official languages. Many of these youth still believe themselves to be full members of a First Nation society. They are Aboriginals, but they differ slightly in thought and practice from their parents and grandparents, just as the ancestors of their parents and grandparents differed from their predecessors.

Some Indian languages are currently being taught in public schools as heritage languages for example, German, Hungarian, Polish, or Ukrainian. Saskatchewan has become the lead province in developing a centralized Aboriginal language curriculum for primary and secondary schools (Fettes and Norton, 2000: 47). This is a positive step because it will, hopefully, give opportunity for nonNatives to expand the repertoire of their potential language learning. At that point they may be able to appreciate some of the nuances of traditional Native thought and even adopt some of the values implicit in Aboriginal language. Such a development may lead to a deeper level of appreciation for the ancient ways of Canada's First Peoples.

The inclusion of Native languages in public school curricula will only happen if the First Nations' lobby actively promotes it. These are, after all, *Aboriginal* languages, not European languages. No one can appreciate that fact more than Indigenous people themselves, and no one can do a better selling job of it than they. Native language promotion is a vital plank in the program of Aboriginal integration defined in this discussion, and the challenge to support such an undertaking lies uniquely within the Native community itself.

Acknowledging Learning Styles

As every teacher knows, individual students learn in individual ways, and sensitive teachers will adapt their teaching methods to suit the needs of individual students. This is naturally easier said than done, particularly with 20 or more students in a classroom. When cultural variations are added to the mix, the situation becomes even more challenging. Stairs (1995) emphasizes the point that the traditional First Nations' style of teaching/learning is significantly different than the EuroCanadian style. Native learners typically develop concepts and skills by repeating tasks in many varying situations instead of in a classroom laboratory setting. The focus in the teaching/learning process is on values and identity, and developed through the learner's relationship to significant others and to the environment. Verbalization of a concept will not be as important as the student's ability to enact the inherent process. Emphasis will be on the student's ability to perform without necessarily being able to provide a step-by-step analysis of it.

One of the primary differences between traditional Native ways of teaching/learning and the contemporary EuroCanadian style has to do with individuality. While both traditions make claims about respecting individuality, Native communities respect individual differences within the bounds of cultural norms. Young learners are accepted as individuals, and are afforded a great deal of leeway in developing themselves. They are not expected to progress in the same direction or at the same rate of speed as their peers, and when their talents have been developed, they are expected to benefit the community. By contrast, nonNative children seem to be unaware of their network of social roles and the orienting social context surrounding the skills and information they are acquiring in school. They do not internalize what they have learned until it is confirmed either by passing an examination or by obtaining approval from a teacher (Stairs, 1995: 143).

Hodgeson-Smith (2000) describes Native students as field-dependent learners, which means that they are more apt to depend on confronting situations when inculcating knowledge. Thus they tend to show a preference for precise guided assignments, and indicate a greater need for a variety of different classroom interaction patterns than their nonNative peers. They also prefer more frequent student-teacher interactions, are more peer-oriented, and more positively inclined towards collaborative and small-group learning tasks.

Significant differences in behavior often come into play when teachers and students represent different cultural backgrounds. At the same time such situations can furnish enriching learning opportunities for both parties. Stairs (1995) makes the point that nonNative teachers working in Indian communities should see themselves as cultural brokers because they select and transmit to Native students aspects of the culture they represent. The role of broker involves the dual responsibility of looking to students for clues, while simultaneously searching the system itself for modifications to allow more appropriate responses to Aboriginal students. A related challenge exists for First Nations teachers working in their home communities. They too will find themselves serving as cultural brokers in seeking to discovering a balance between the divergent goals of education in preparing students for jobs and for effective functioning within their own cultural configuration (Stairs, 1995: 147).

Culturally-Relevant Curriculum

There are radical differences between the way Aboriginal people traditionally taught their young and the way contemporary schools are supposed to be doing the job. Before European contact, Indian children "learned on the job." The emphasis was on observation, modelling, and individual experience. Aboriginal children watched their parents and emulated them, much in the way that all rural families, Native and nonNative, passed on their valued behaviors and skills in early Canada. They participated in so-called adult activities at a relatively young age so they could get the feel of the activity. The specialty of the traditional First Nations' educational style was that it rested on entirely unique philosophical/spiritual grounds. The Indigenous peoples saw the universe as a whole; everything was connected, and all living things–people, animals, and plants – were perceived as "all my relations." There were no separate subdivisions of thought such as biological, mental, spiritual, or psychological. The curriculum studied by First Nations children brought everything together, encompassed within a spiritual blanket. Every act, every behavior, was seen as having spiritual implications in that it reflected on the individual's earthly journey. How the individual reacted to each momentary experience was an indication of his or her interpretation of why they had been placed on earth by the Creator.

When contrasted with the imported European model of schooling, significant differences could be noted. The newly-arrived missionary teachers were not so much interested in identifying individual interpretations of perceived phenomena as they were in dictating to children what they had to know and how they had to act. The universe was not viewed by these teachers as a unified whole but as a metaphysical laboratory with distinct subdivisions – biological, mental, psychological, and, to a lesser extent, spiritual.

The mentality that knowledge can analytically be dissected pervades schools to this day with the exception that all references to spiritual aspects of living have been eliminated. In many Canadian schools today it is not even permissable to allude to Canada's Christian heritage (even at Christmas) lest someone from another country or faith be offended. We are now apparently a multicultural country with no particular religious or spiritual history or previous philosophical allegiance. With the elimination of any references to the spiritual domain in school programs, small wonder that many First Nations students do not do well. According to what they learn in their home communities, spirituality is the primary foundation for all learning. In truly modern Canadian schools they are being told that spirituality is a private matter to be practiced outside of school hours, and then probably only on Sundays.

Substituting or adding Aboriginal emphases to school curricula may not be as simple a procedure as at first appears. Indian bands generally vary somewhat in belief and practice even if they are part of the same culture area. Not all plains tribes believe or practice their culture in the same manner. This is particularly true for West Coast Indigenous cultures, Plateau Indians, northern First Nations, or Woodland peoples. Even local Aboriginal communities or bands, who may be members of a larger First Nations cultural configuration, may differ slightly in their lifestyle from their tribal counterparts. Teachers working in these respective areas will need to keep their ears tuned to what is acceptable in each community. Increased awareness of the various elements of local community life can potentially lead to the development of more culturally appropriate teaching styles and materials.

When Native communities embark on local curriculum development, they face a complex challenge. The first step is usually to obtain funding for the project and get their constituents to appreciate the worthiness of the concept. Then individuals representing the various community sectors will be invited to an introductory meeting. When this happens it becomes necessary to outline the task and ascertain if consensus on objectives can be attained. Not everyone will readily buy into the process; some individuals may participate in such activities strictly for the social benefits they offer. After all, it is good to get together with friends (Archibald, 1995: 297).

Obtaining community consensus on curriculum development is not necessarily an easy task. Because of the impact of assimilative influences in many communities, Native parents and leaders have different perspectives on appropriate subject content in school. There are also differences in values and language usage. Some Indigenous parents would like to see their children taught strictly in the old ways while others see the need for them to be able to function effectively in both Native and nonNative worlds. There may even be a few individuals who might lean more towards a contemporary curricular emphasis in their local school. Language variations may emerge over time as differences in usage occur among the various bands within a given Native community. Obviously consensus on language form needs to be achieved if a standardized curriculum is to be developed (Morris and Price, 1991).

The primary objective for local curriculum development is to provide a means by which Aboriginal students can learn about their historical backgrounds within the school context. The belief is that this will help students gain a more positive self-image and thus improve learning. It may also serve to develop an increased awareness and more positive attitude toward their cultural affiliation. At the same time, Aboriginal curriculum designers are well aware that any modifications they undertake cannot in any way deprive students of the opportunity to develop usable skills for today's job market. Generally speaking, local curriculum changes in First Nations' communities have served to bolster student confidence as well as enhance student marketable skills.

Curriculum revisions logically necessitate new forms of teacher training for both elders who will participate in teaching as well as certified classroom teachers. For the latter group this may require two significant adjustments, one in regard to familiarizing themselves with new content, and the other with regard to shifting teaching/learning procedures. The involvement of elders in the teaching process has been one of the highlights of Aboriginal curriculum development. Elders are finding that the contemporary classroom is quite different than the classic traditional Aboriginal scene in which their predecessors used to gather children in a circle around them and tell them stories. This reality makes it essential that elders become part of the training process along with regular classroom teachers. There is reason to believe that an open attitude on the part of both parties toward such opportunity can be a mutually-beneficial, culturally-enriching experience.

While Native children are currently gaining exposure to the history and culture of their ancestors, there is also a need for nonNative children to learn about traditional Indigenous ways. Public school curricula should incorporate Native-produced materials so that students can study the viewpoints of Aboriginal writers on vital subjects. Too much of Indian content produced by departments of education today is shallow, patronizing, and often erroneous, while it glosses over significant events and cultural themes from a EuroCanadian viewpoint. Aboriginal produced curricula provide a balance by demonstrating another perspective. After all, with the strong emphasis in schools today on studying all aspects of a given subject, and then making up one's own mind, it behooves school systems to provide alternative interpretations of all kinds of happenings and phenomena. Incorporating First Nations-produced materials could go a long way toward such an end and place a stamp of approval on what has been held up as an admirable multicultural approach.

Incorporating Indigenous Knowledge

The dual traditions of Native Americans and Europeans have been juxtaposed on this continent for half a millennium. Although many adherents to the latter view perceived that soon after their arrival in North America the Indigenous peoples would be assimilated into the European way of thinking, this has not occurred. The truth is that Aboriginal peoples have experienced severe repercussions from the cultural clash, but many of their ways have

and training, and what will be its source and content? By now most Native communities are so besieged by outside forces, and so infiltrated by EuroCanadian values and ideas, that any attempt to "purify" Aboriginal knowledge will be a near impossibility. It is not even certain that the majority of Indigenous peoples, particularly younger generations, desire that to happen. The fact is that two-thirds of Canada's Status Indians live off reserve, many of them in urban areas where they are subject to the most influential EuroCanadian ways of thinking and behaving. Perhaps the best that can occur is a synthesis of the two traditions, shaped and modified according to specifications fashioned by the Native majority.

Ermine (1995: 102) posits three specific orientations that Indigenous people must promote in order to transform society to appreciate the old ways. These are: (i) teaching the skills that promote personal and social transformation; (ii) providing a vision of social change that lead to harmony with rather than control over the environment; and, (iii) continuing to attribute a spiritual dimension to the environment.

Weber-Pillwax (1999) expands this concern towards those who undertake research in Aboriginal communities and suggests adherence to the following principles in building an Indigenous research methodology. *First*, is the notion of interconnectedness in Indigenous philosophy. All forms of living are to be respected as being related and interconnected. This means that transformation is to be anticipated within every living thing participating in the research program. *Second*, researchers must assure themselves that all motives for doing research will result in benefits to the Indigenous community. *Third*, the foundation for Indigenous research must lie within the reality of the lived Indigenous experience. *Fourth*, any theories developed or proposed will need to be grounded in and supported by Indigenous epistemology. *Fifth*, the languages and cultures of Indigenous people must be perceived as living processes, and scholars should realize that any research carried on within the Indigenous community can contribute towards the creation of knowledge. This fact necessitates the participation of Aboriginal people in any research involving their communities.

The Indigenous assignment will not readily be endorsed in a society that stresses perpetual exploitation of the earth's resources (Friedel, 1999). Most North Americans believe that the universe can be understood and controlled through atomism. As Ermine (1995: 102) states, "The intellectual tendency in Western science is the acquisition and synthesis of total human knowledge within a world-view that seeks to understand the outer space objectively." This view effectively eliminates delving into the spiritual domain because it is not perceived as having been objectively constructed. By denying the reality of spirituality, modern science has produced a fragmented view of humankind and shut down the possibility of benefitting from the knowledge of Indigenous elders – "those who know" (Kirk, 1986). By contrast, traditional societies have always relied first of all on the wisdom of elders and holy people who carefully safeguarded and taught the spiritual secrets of the universe to succeeding generations.

As the sages of Old Testament times intoned:

> There is wisdom, remember, in age, and a long life brings understanding. (Job 12:12)
> Walk with the wise and be wise; mix with the stupid and be misled. (Proverbs 13:20 NEB)

Thus any informational campaign undertaken by the Native community will necessarily include an attachment about appreciating the richness of years of human experience.

Three

Traditional Aboriginal Philosophy

Native leaders are generally agreed that education is the key that will open the door of the future for Canada's Aboriginal people. For many years, however, the voice of the First Nations has been silenced due to the nature of education which they endured. For a long time children of First Nations were exposed to an educational system under the auspices of the Indian Act whereby the federal government assumed complete control of the children and their schooling. The consequences of this arrangement resulted in mind transformation instead of individual development. Eventually the process of cognitive imperialism had a crushing effect on Native communities. Several generations of Aboriginals lost their world-views, languages, and cultures and were forced to live with psychological and social upheaval. This scene is about to change as First Nations communities determine what the nature of their education should be.

Until quite recently, most books about Canadian or United States history either disregarded any happenings before the European invasion of this continent, or only alluded to them in passing. In Canada most historians dealt primarily with matters pertaining directly to the dealings of the Charter Nations (English and French), and anything connected to First Nations communities was relegated second place status, if even acknowledged. Today the scene is changing, thanks largely to the work of Indigenous writers, particularly Native historians such as Olive Dickason (1984, 1993), a retired University of Alberta professor. Canadian history now reaches back before the time of Jacques Cartier and includes developments in arenas beyond that of the Charter Nations.

Being strongly ethnocentric in perspective, early Canadian historians found it quite easy to ignore many precontact historical developments in North America. Partially this was because these writers were not trained to appreciate the nuances or validity of the oral tradition which was central to the First Nations way of life. Coupled with this was the complicating factor of Native spirituality which framed the foundation of oral transmission. A sad omission that, because discovery and comprehension of the depth and dimensions of the oral tradition make it possible to appreciate the rudiments of the first extensive educational system on this continent (Friesen, 2000: 113f).

The antiquated view that the Aboriginal way of thinking is inferior to its EuroAmerican counterpart is slowly eroding. Scholars are beginning to discover that previous methods of studying diverse knowledge forms are often unreliable, and a new broadmindedness is emerging in academic circles. No longer are varying epistemologies being subjected to western tests of coherence and correspondence, but instead new approaches to knowledge gathering and understanding, such as hermeneutical phenomenology, are being developed. The misguided theory which suggests that primitive mankind once took up the pursuit of knowledge at the bottom of some kind of scale and worked up to the sophistication of modern times (Morgan, 1963: 3), is now gathering dust on library shelves.

A century ago, many anthropologists still promulgated the ancient notion that societal progress was intricately connected to technology. Until quite recently, it was widely believed that the progressive development of inventions, discoveries, and institutions supported the notion that since the origin of the humans, their aggressive efforts helped them ascend to a higher rung on the ladder of evolutionary civilization. This perspective was premised on the European-inherited notion that the tribal societies encountered by the first visitors to North America were vastly inferior to those they had left behind in Spain, France, or England. Morgan (1963) cited seven proofs of the latter's success including more finely developed forms of subsistence, government, speech, family, religion and architecture, and the origin of the notion of property ownership.

Traditional Eurocentric thinkers enunciated the view that the Aryan kinship family enjoyed "intrinsic superiority" when compared with the First Peoples of North America (Battiste and Henderson, 2000). This implied mental and moral inferiority on the part of the Indigenous peoples due to cultural underdevelopment and inexperience hindered by animal appetites and passions. Small wonder that the Aboriginal tribal configurations encountered by the first Europeans in North American were immediately denigrated and assigned inferior status. The imported philosophers boasted that the vast "improvements" of modern society, particularly the quest for property ownership, could even produce unmanageable power quests that would surely be the unmaking of civilization. It was further projected that the attainment of the highest plane of civilization that could be envisaged, might imply a return to the ancient ways that respected liberty, equality, and fraternity. This future state was not to be confused with savage or barbaric communalism, because tribal configurations could at best hold such ideals in embryonic form (Dippie, 1985: 110).

The emergence of some form of ideal state may yet become reality. The tendency to respect the earth and all living things once so clearly exhibited by tribal societies is today being hailed as an urgent need. John Collier, Indian Commissioner for the United States, once commented on the traditional Indigenous reverence for the earth, "They [the First Nations] had what the world has lost. They have it now. What the world has lost the world must have again, lest it die" (Bordewich, 1996: 71). Some philosophers, like Knudtson and Suzuki (1992), are optimistic in observing that increasing numbers of people are beginning to recognize the degree of respect afforded the earth by many ancient societies must be regained – and soon. They maintain that

> If biodiversity and ecosystem integrity are critical to salvaging some of the skin of life on earth, then every successful fight to protect the land of Indigenous Peoples is a victory for all humanity and for all living things. (Knudtson and Suzuki, 1992: xxxiv)

Knudtson and Suzuki go on to argue that the ecological impact of industrial civilization, and the sheer weight of human numbers, is now a global concern because these realities are changing the biosphere with frightening speed. It is clear that such problems as global warming, species depletion, ozone depletion and pollution cannot be resolved by any band-aid approach such as higher taxes, government intervention or recycling. A radical approach that consists of new ways of relating to the universe is both urgent and necessary. If this truth ever sinks in there may be a scramble to understand why the ancients prized the forces of nature so highly.

There is a prophecy among the Lakota Sioux that eventually people of other races and cultures will come to the First Nations seeking the wisdom of their elders. The next generation may realize they are out of balance with the universe and out of right relation with the Great Mystery and Grandmother earth despite their many packed houses of worship. Future generations of Indians must therefore be prepared to help them when they come. It will be a time of renewal (Kaltreider, 1998: 91).

Aboriginal Origins

Scientists on the edge always seem to have an explanation for the unknown, often in the form of an unsupported theory without which nothing apparently seems to make sense. This is certainly true in regard to the history of North American First Nations whose ancestors are often labelled Paleo Indians or Clovis People by anthropologists. About the best explanation of their ancient lifestyle that can be rendered is the conjecture that the people were big-game hunters and gatherers. As Bowden (1981: 3) notes:

> We know nothing about the clothing, shelters, or social organization of the peoples who constituted this tradition and very little about their appearance, values, and religious orientation.

This admission has not hindered the speculative process, which, in fairness, is not entirely without some evidence. Several excavated archaeological sites have verified the theory about the existence of big-game. A recent dig at Big Springs, South Dakota, for example, has substantiated the previous existence of several species of mammals whose perfectly-preserved skeletons were discovered in a sink-hole where these creatures perished when they came to drink. The bones of one species of mammals found in the sink-hole show them to have measured nearly five metres (over fourteen feet) in height.

It is heartening to note that social scientists are gradually eliminating ethnocentric comments while studying First Nations' cultures, and producing works more readily oriented towards the acknowledgment of Aboriginal contributions to the North American way of life. Several decades ago, anthropologists, like Ruth Underhill (1953), still clung tenaciously to the theory that Indigenous peoples migrated to North American via the Bering Strait. Driver (1969: 4) was more hesitant stating; "Although we are certain that there was some contact between South Pacific Islands and South America before 1492, this came much too late to account for any principal peopling of the New World."

The lack of information about the fabled Bering Strait theory did not keep anthropologists from guessing about Native origins on this continent. The general presupposition on which the Bering Strait theory was promulgated was that since archaeological evidence exists to identify the presence of Indigenous peoples 11 000 years ago in the Valley of Mexico, this means that their ancestors must have come to America via the Bering Strait thousands of years earlier. Today, anyone reading Vine Deloria, Jr.'s sarcastic repudiation of that theory is sure to agree with him that "the Bering Strait theory is simply shorthand scientific language for, 'I don't know, but it sounds good and no one will check'" (Deloria, 1995: 81). Sadly, if Deloria is correct, the most compelling reason for advancing the theory is to justify European colonization. If it can convincingly be argued that First Nations were also recent immigrants to North America, they would lose their claim to being original inhabitants and the right of first occupancy.

Gradually descriptions about Indian migrations have begun to take on a degree of sophistication, but musings about the Bering Strait linger. As Owen, Deetz and Fisher have suggested;

> The dates of the earliest migration to the New World are still in question. . . . Regarded as even less likely are those fanciful contentions which suggest that the origin of American Indians can be attributed to sunken continents or wandering lost tribes. (Owen, Deetz, and Fisher, 1968: 3)

Josephy was more specific, and estimates that the bridge across the Bering Strait was probably part of the path that led to the New World some 12 000 to 35 000 years ago (Josephy, 1968: 37). Peter Farb (1968: 191) concurred, but estimated that proof exists to show that Aboriginal people had lived on this continent at least 13 000 years ago. Jennings (1978: 1) was even more persistent, insisting that "There is no reasonable doubt as to the ultimate origin of the human population that finally covered the hemisphere. There is consensus among scholars that the first American was of Asian stock." Deloria was right; for "professionals" of this ilk, any form of "educated" speculation would appear to be much superior to what they might term pure fantasy, although the differences might not be evident to anyone else.

Regardless of specificity of origin, it is becoming evident that before European contact, Aboriginal peoples of the various culture areas in North America lived full and probably satisfying lives. They had plenty of food and there were thriving agricultural communities around the Great Lakes Region, in the Eastern Woodlands, in the southwest, and as far north as North Dakota. Fishing was a major source of food supply on both east and west coasts as well as among the Plateau Indians in what is now the British Columbia Interior. When the Woodland Peoples migrated to the plains several centuries ago they developed a nomadic lifestyle following the migration patterns of the buffalo. The base of all of these cultures rested on a philosophy of ready adjustment to changes necessitated by natural forces. Many of the more sedentary civilizations left impressive remains behind which gave a clear indication of the extent of their technological genius. The moundbuilders of the American southeast bequeathed thousands of huge temple mounds as well as burial and effigy mounds, some of which had lunar alignments (Shaffer, 1992). The Anasazi of the southwest left huge walled cities, some of them five stories high. Their neighbors, the Hohokam, dug hundreds of miles of water-carrying canals, many of which are still in use today. Only the plains tribes left little physical evidence of the magnitude and genius of their cultures save for buffalo jumps and remains of winter camps and other sites of interest to archaeologists.

Using these remains as foundation for their theories, social scientists have tried to reconstruct the rudiments of past cultures. Unfortunately, they too often disregarded the oral tradition in constructing their prototypes. We can learn from their mistakes by incorporating elements of existing Indigenous knowledge into planning for the future.

Tribal World-View

It is useful for researchers to note that many Aboriginal societies today much more resemble the lifestyles of their forebears than do those social systems that were imported from Europe. The genius of this reality is that it is still possible to study and comprehend the workings of Indigenous societies in that they reflect the essence of their traditional ways. In addition, the cultural revitalization movement that is active among First Peoples today has placed new emphasis on old ways so that elders are being sought out to explain the old ways and bring them back into practice. Many ancient customs and rituals that were once deemed lost are being reenacted with new meaning as elders begin to share their knowledge. Fortunately, these have not been stamped out, for many of them were simply taken underground and held there until the time was right to release them. Illustrative of the rebirth of Aboriginal ceremonies include the sundance, potlatch, pipe ceremonies, use of sweetgrass, transfer ceremonies, and a host of other rituals (Lincoln: 1985).

Some 19th century anthropologists made the unfortunate ethnocentric error of assuming that cultural change always implies improvement. They also assumed that the Eurocentric model of cultural development could well serve as an international, indeed global model of human achievement, and should be copied by civilizations everywhere. A reexamination of this rather haughty perspective has convinced even anthropologists that they may have been too hasty in denouncing Aboriginal tribal cultures as inferior.

Many social and spiritual aspects of pre-contact tribal cultures are now coming to light, thanks to the willingness of Native elders to open the vaults of Indigenous knowledge (Couture, 1991a). In light of these admissions, there is reason to believe that Aboriginal peoples from many different areas on this continent traditionally ascribed to a similar metaphysical perspective while it remained unaffected by immigration, industry or imported forms of technology. It is necessary, of course, to acknowledge the diversity that existed among traditional Indian cultures with respect to their means of obtaining food, cultural practices, lifestyle, and so on, but the basic theological system to which they all subscribed was fundamentally tribal.

The need for this discussion stems from the fact that while the *Weltanschauung* of the First Peoples is markedly different than that of EuroCanadians; it is simply a significantly different way of viewing the world. An examination of four traditional core values which are still well-preserved among many Native tribes will substantiate this assertion.

(1) A Holistic, Global Perspective

> Nature prevailed and flourished for untold centuries, unchanged by the Indian. – Chief Red Fox, Sioux First Nation (Friesen, 1998: 8)

> Canadians are a lucky people. Nature's lottery has left us with undant natural resources, oil and gas among them. But we are also a careless people. Rich in resources, we have been poor in policy. – David Crane, columnist, *Controlling Interest: The Canadian Gas and Oil Stakes.* (Colombo, 1987: 250)

It is difficult for nonAboriginals to comprehend the implications of a holistic view of the universe, but the Indigenous peoples traditionally believed that all phenomena, including both material and non-material elements, are connected and interconnected. The interconnectedness of all things on earth means that everything we do has consequences that reverberate through the system of which we are a part (Suzuki, 1997: 102). Native people do not adhere to any "scientific" breakdown of how people function or how the universe operates. The nonNative scientific view further allows and encourages the development of separate "hard-core" academic disciplines which seek to identify and explain the various components of cosmic and material phenomena, such as biophysics, astrochemistry, biotechnology, nuclear mathematics, social physiology, and so on. Although the proponents of each of these specialties will make sophisticated claims about interdisciplinary parallels and concerns, there is always an element of professional ethnocentrism involved in their scientific deliberations.

This delineation of disciplinary specialties is quite foreign to the First Nations way of thinking. Aboriginal People view the world as an interconnected series of only sometimes distinguishable or comprehensible elements. They experience no uneasiness at the thought of multiple realities simultaneously operant in the universe, and they do not differentiate among the varieties or qualities of entities, that is between material or spiritual elements. Their world-view allows for the possibility that a variety of "structurally-different" elements may simultaneously be active in the process of holistic healing. This also explains why dreams, visions, and personal experiences comprise as important a source of knowledge as scientifically-derived truths. In short, you never know where you might gain knowledge or where you might learn something.

Indian tribal appreciation for the spiritual dimension has been underestimated and misunderstood by researchers from the time of first contact. Not recognizing the nature of Indian spirituality, since the Europeans had left their own tribal origins far behind, the newcomers underestimated the extent to which spiritual concerns were valued by Native peoples as a significant part of daily life. In fact, the invaders assumed that the Indians were not even spiritually-oriented in the conventional sense. At most Indigenous People were accused of worshipping "evil spirits." European thinkers tended to place great importance on institutionalized religion which was routinely delineated in terms of elaborately-decorated physical structures and structured procedures. From the European perspective there were few meaningful points by which to compare the two systems. In an interesting twist, the clash of the two traditions produced a regrettable functionality of sorts. European spokespersons, particularly those backed by a religious hierarchy, believed in making authoritative claims about the various workings of the universe. Indians, on the other hand, were a listening people; if anyone did make such a claim, he or she was certainly given an audience because not to do so might be to risk losing valuable insights. After all, no one would knowingly make a false claim about having a particular spiritual insight because the fear of being exposed was strong. An individual's claim to truth was expected to be validated through subsequent happenings. After contact the arrangement was that the claim-making newcomers gained a dominant position in negotiations based on their particular interpretation of who was in possession of a superior theological system.

The traditional Native tribal orientation towards the universe naturally blossomed into a resignation to work with forces of the universe. The power of these forces was obvious, yet rhythmic, and by respecting these reliable patterns, it was possible to sustain a form of cultural life on earth. A further extension of this mind-set was an inherent warning not to seek to dominate or exploit nature, but always to work in harmony with it.

Tribal cultures have always had a profound respect for the earth, largely because they appreciated its produce for sustenance. As Leobold notes,

> The land is not merely soil; it is a foundation of energy flowing through a circuit of souls, plants and animals . . . An ethic to supplement and guide the economic relation to land presupposes the existence of some mental image of land as a biotic mechanism. We can be ethical only in relation to something we can see, feel, understand, love, or otherwise have faith in. (quoted in Suzuki, 1997: 104)

The concept of personal or group ownership of land was foreign to Indian tribal societies at the time of treaty-signing. Their concept of a treaty was one of creating a good and lasting friendship between two nations who at one time were at war with one another or who wanted to avoid war. When the Canadian government began the process of signing written treaties in 1871 with First Nations across the country, they were building on a process that was quite familiar to the Aboriginal peoples. Most tribes had a long history of treaty-making with other nations, usually negotiated as a symbol of peace, and accompanied by the ceremonial smoking of the pipe and the exchange of gifts. To Native people, smoking the pipe was analogous to the nonNative practice of swearing on the Bible (Treaty 7, 1996: 68). Some historians also estimate that before 1871 when the formal treaty-signing process began, as many as 500 treaties had been signed between First Nations and European governments. Unlike the numbered treaties, the previous treaties were primarily friendship agreements intended to hinder the outbreak of war. To this day many Native leaders regret that their forebears were forced to give up their lands when they participated in treaty signing.

Traditionally, tribal societies relied on the oral tradition for passing along revered cultural knowledge. This was done largely through storytelling. The oral tradition afforded an entirely flexible dimension to tribal philosophy with the inbuilt possibility of reacting to unexpected changes much in the way that nature does. Contrasted with the current preoccupation for recording everything, an Oglala elder, Four Guns, once stated:

> Many of the white man's ways are past our understanding . . . They put a great store upon writing; there is always a paper.
>
> The white people must think paper has some mysterious power to help them in the world. The Indian needs no writings; words that are true sink deep into his heart, where they remain. He never forgets them. On the other hand, if the white man loses his paper, he is helpless.
>
> I once heard one of their preachers say that no white man was admitted to heaven unless there were writings about him in a great book! (Friesen, 1995a: 38)

In the traditional First Nations' world there was only one universal and absolute truth – the universe exists and its rhythms must be respected. Often described in terms such as respect for nature or working in harmony with nature, the underlying truth requires is worthy of greater analysis. Coupled with the concept of interconnectedness the universe remains the object of reverence albeit veiled in mystery. There are no satisfying scientific explanations in this approach, and the deeper mysteries are only partially understood through non-scientific, spiritual truths or through mythology steeped in time.

Belief in the eternal mystique of the universe prohibits the idea of exploitation or domination. An unknowable and hallowed entity should not be approached in any other manner but with respect, awe, and obeisance. One should not tamper with the elements or workings of the universe, but respect its modus operandi. As the mysterious but Divinely-controlled source of life and sustenance the earth's power is enigmatic but reliable. To question or seek to tamper with its rhythmic functions would be tantamount to playing God.

Pelletier (Frideres, 1974: 105-106), describes the difference between an Indian and nonIndian approach to the universe in a scene that places him on the top of a mountain in British Columbia. There he imagines he has been assigned the awesome responsibility of improving his natural environment. His first inclination is to stock the sky with a few more birds or perhaps move a few clouds around to provide balance. Then his eye falls on an old plank lying on the ground at his feet and he decides to relocate it to a more appropriate place. The plank is obviously hindering the grass from growing. As he lifts the plank he notices that the underside of it contains a whole colony of insect life. Ants are scrambling to move their eggs to safety, woodlice are digging to get down into the ground, earthworms are coiled up like snakes, and a spider is staring him straight in the face demanding, "What have you done to my world?" Pelletier immediately puts the board down as close to the original place as possible, and apologizes to the insects for disturbing their society. Then he gives thanks for the lesson that he is being taught not to interfere with the doings of the universe (Pelletier, 1974).

Tribal cultures all around the world once respected the natural workings of the earth, but once the infusion of industrialization and technology was realized, this ethic became frustrated. True, some of the inventions of the new outlook proved satisfying and convenient, but the effect on the environment was beyond comprehension. In the conquering mode of today's urban development campaign, the mandate is still to rearrange the earth in a pattern that is virtually indistinguishable when compared with the previous format; nothing can remain untouched, if not completely destroyed. This, after all, is progress. Imagine a traditionally-minded Aboriginal bystander solemnly pondering the process, wondering if "progress" will eventually run its course and Mother Earth be allowed to resume her natural course.

Soon after government negotiators completed the signing of Treaty 7 with the Blood Tribe of southern Alberta, officials suggested that the tribe consider selling off some of their land to provide revenue. This idea was greeted by one chief's unequivocal announcement, "The grass is for sale, but not the earth." Implicit in this pronouncement was the belief that the resources of Mother Earth were for everyone's benefit but the earth itself should not be divided up for private ownership or for personal gain.

The downside of earth reverence, if it may be so labelled, is that the resultant attitude towards the universe can take many forms. The strong penchant toward "earth maintenance," so strongly valued by many successors of the European tradition, for example, might be viewed by Native people as comprising a form of tampering with the operations of the universe. Nowhere is there a better illustration of this than when formerly-developed modern communities wither and fall into disuse. Abandoned town-sites serve to substantiate the Indian view that nonNative people tend to build and abandon or destroy. They dig basements, erect buildings, lay paved roads and streets, and install elaborate underground wiring and pipe systems. The result is a modern community. When a town dies, however, in many cases the modern trappings of convenience are left to decay, often inflicting permanent damage to the environment as well as comprising an eye-sore (even by nonNative standards). Native people find this situation quite incomprehensible. In their view, in time, happily the earth will return to find its own level – provided that no irreparable damage has been done in the meantime.

The First Nations of North America see themselves as part of a great chain of existence that includes all aspects of creation; all elements in this natural chain are interrelated and interdependent. If any single element is subjected to undue attention or pressure or is tampered with, there will be repercussions in the grand scheme of things. Scientists may wish to argue with this layman's view of things, because the western perspective conceives of the universe in terms of chains of cause-and-effect. Things are what they are, and do what they do, largely because antecedent things did what they did and were what they were. The underlying assumption is that if we design the right tools and approaches we will be able to understand those chains of cause-and-effect and perhaps tailor them to our own objectives. However, when one ponders the tremendous changes that have occurred in society in recent decades, which have necessarily impacted on the environment, the mind boggles. If the earth has been a working enterprise for "millions of years" as we have been led to believe by those same scientists, even a non-scientist can imagine what the effect of increased chemical use and pollution – of the earth, air and water – might be to the universe. This damage to the universe has been accomplished in only a few years, which amounts to a relatively insignificant hiccup in light of the duration of the earth's existence. It may not be true that every irregularity caused by a scientific adjustment can also be rectified by still another scientific adjustment. If this is so, surely the matter is at least cause for serious concern if not diligent study.

Warnings about this state of affairs are inherent in traditional Indigenous knowledge. If ever there was a need to integrate this knowledge into the public domain, it is now. The call for Aboriginal elders to speak out has never been more urgent.

(2) An Appreciation for Life and Family

When you arise in the morning, give thanks for the light; give thanks for the morning, for life and strength; Give thanks for your food and the joy of living. If you see no reason for giving thanks, rest assured, the fault lies within yourself. – Chief Tecumseh, Shawnee First Nation (Friesen, 1998: 14)

Think of yourself as a human being; and you cannot help feeling the reality of life around you, and becoming impregnated with it.
– Paraskeva Clark, artist, "Come Out from Behind the PreCambrian Shield," New Frontier. (Colombo, 1987: 207)

If anyone does not provide for his relatives, and especially for his immediate family, he has denied the faith and is worse than an unbeliever. (I Timothy 5:8 NIV)

One of the hardest "truths" for addicts of the work-ethic to accept is for anyone to claim that work of itself has no virtue. Although this orientation is rapidly changing, due to increased mechanization, few contemporary EuroCanadians probably need to be coaxed into believing in the value of work. By contrast, an important underlying presupposition of the traditional Native lifestyle was to shun work for its own sake, and even demean any colleague who might have such leanings. Virtue was seen as emanating from living in the "perennial now," and staying to remain in tune with one's spiritual destiny. Staying alive was a principal occupation of ancient tribal societies and it was accomplished via hunting and gathering, through agriculture or via a combination of these activities. For hunting societies, it was necessary to pursue game only when the larder was empty. Once the larder was full, due to the results of a successful hunt, it was time to celebrate.

The First Nations' attitude towards work originated in a present-oriented, survival-centred society. Game was hunted to fulfil present needs, and with the exception of being stored as pemmican, meat could not be preserved for long periods of time. When the circumstances of hunting and gathering called for hard work, it was done, but there was no concept of holding a job in order to be "doing something" or as a means of validating one's existence. Work was undertaken to fulfil a specific task or to satisfy a pressing need –

nothing more. The Indigenous people had great faith in the Creator's miraculous provision.

An intriguing procedure by which to obtain necessary food was once practiced among the Mandan Indians of what is now North Dakota. Although primarily an agricultural people, the Mandans and their neighbours, the Arikara, and Hidatsa, also hunted buffalo. Being a sedentary society, however, they did not always find it convenient to engage in long distance hunting. They preferred not to wander too far way from their homes and leave them unguarded. As a result they invented the "buffalo calling ceremony" which was usually held during the winter months in hopes of luring the bison near to their villages. During the ceremony, which was presided over by the elders, the entire village became quiet. Dogs were muzzled and children were appeased with whatever it took to keep them quiet. Then everyone waited for the buffalo to come close to the village. Usually the plan worked, assuring the people that they were indeed being looked after by the Creator (Schneider, 1989: 62).

The Native concept of work correlates with the contemporary misguided notion of "Indian time." Observers often joke about "Indian time" as though to imply that First Nations are always late. The truth of the matter is that Indians are sometimes late (at least by nonNative standards), and sometimes they do not even show up for an appointment when they are expected to do so. Of course there are also many nonNatives whose actions fit this description. This does not mean that a sense of time is always irrelevant, but rather that time per se is not the only nor necessarily the most important criterion by which to determine how a particular moment ought to be acted out. It is certainly not a top priority of itself. There are times when Indian people are actually early, depending on circumstances or purpose and the relative importance of an event. Above all, clock-watching per se simply does not happen. It is basically an irrelevant (and perhaps irreverent) entity in the Aboriginal scheme of things.

Traditionally, all tribal societies lived in tune with the cycles of nature. Living off the land and depending on its rhythms meant that nature dictated when things would happen. No one went out to collect blueberries or other edibles until they had ripened to the optimal degree. Nor did they trap until the time of year when pelts were at their fullest. Crops were harvested when they were ready, not on a certain date. While they waited the hunters prepared or repaired their equipment and planned their strategies (Ross, 1992: 39). Thus the notion of "the time being right" is a principle embedded in the very nature of things; to dance to the tune of a different drummer would be foolish. Like other tribal societies, First Nations well recognized who was in control of the elements. They reverently respected the Creator and were well aware of the consequences of neglecting His dictates. This is aptly illustrated in the reminder given to the Old Testament Bible Prophet, Amos:

> . . . I also withheld rain from you when the harvest was still three months away. I sent rain on one town but withheld it from another. One field had rain; another had none and dried up. People staggered from town to town for water but did not get enough to drink, yet you have not returned to me, declares the Lord. (Amos 4:7-8 NIV)

One of the most amazing contradictions of modern society is the claim that family, particularly immediate family, is a top priority when it is obvious that almost everything else takes precedence. This is particularly true when it comes to personal fulfilment through vocation or career. Often intelligent people are caught singing the praises of family life when in reality they spend only a few minutes per week in meaningful interaction with their children. Often both parents in today's nuclear family aggressively pursue individual careers in order to provide a high level of consumptive lifestyle for their young. This tack is adopted either because both parents believe such to be necessary, or they are simply echoing the "family comes first" slogan which has become quite popular among North American politicians seeking public office.

The strongest unit among most precontact tribal societies was the clan, a linear and usually exogamous kin-group (or sib), often characterized by matrilineal descent. Members of a clan lived together, including all married partners and their children, and were subject to a series of stringent regulations. In addition to being exogamous, clans usually had a set of names reserved for naming offspring, and their own burial ground. They often had special religious symbols, and their religious rites were carried out by specially designated individuals. Clans could adopt outsiders but they too would have to subscribe to clan regulations (Goldenweiser, 1968: 565f). Lowie (1956: 9) points out that among the Crow Indians, who were a matrilineal society, a person was always in the same clan as his or her mother but a man could never belong to the same clan as his children who were born into their mother's group. Even if a father adopted children they automatically fell into the clan of his mother or that of the children's mother. Among the Crows a child could belong to the father's clan only if its mother married a man of her own clan, a practice forbidden by the rules of exogamy.

Clans were (and still are) powerful units among member Nations of the former Iroquois League and the Huron Confederacy. West Coast Indians are also organized according to a highly complex clan system. Migrant Plains Indian tribes traditionally limited themselves to bands of 50 or 100 individuals in order to more easily move camp and follow the buffalo. More sedentary nations like the Arikara, Hidatsa and Mandan, organized larger village settlements of fifty or more lodges, albeit along strict family lines.

The Native orientation towards strong family linkages had many benefits. Child rearing, for example, was a family affair, and a responsibility shared by family and community. Education was ongoing, and consisted of elders telling stories, modelling, and learning by doing (Haig-Brown, 1993: 38). Even today, among some First Nations a significant portion of child-rearing is done by grandparents rather than parents. Often parents are quite young when they have their first child and they usually require advice and assistance. Besides, it is an unspoken rule among Indians that age is correlated with, although not necessarily a direct cause of, wisdom. Grandparents are more settled, more relaxed about life, and therefore they are also more patient in child-raising. This inclination is also characteristic in sibling relationships. Older children in the same classroom are expected to help their younger siblings even though an uninformed nonNative teacher may see such actions as unscrupulous or cheating.

In the context of life and family, First Nations cultures comprised a utopia of sorts. Their priorities were in order, and there was no contradiction between what they claimed and what they lived, clearly an indicator that this value system could again be installed if there was a will to do so. Drawing attention by Aboriginal elders to their precontact functional family life would be in place at this time.

(3) A Caring and Sharing Society

> Material culture is interesting to look at . . . our traditional concept of possessions is not to hoard them, but to use them. If anybody can find a better use for what I have, let him take it. – Russell Wright, Siksika First Nation (Friesen, 1998: 5)

It is a common stereotype to conceive of precontact Indian culture as a sharing society, perhaps because there is truth in the statement. However the meaning of sharing is dependent on the context in which the word is used. In a dictionary definition common to dominant society, "sharing" simply means that those who possess things or have access to resources *may* use those resources to assist others who may be in need. Implicit in the dictionary definition is the assumption that those who have resources may help out the needy if they so choose. The question of wanting to is seldom a relevant factor in Indian culture because of very limited individual choice in the matter.

The Aboriginal twist to the definition of sharing leans quite heavily toward the obligatory component of the process, very much to the point that they who have, *had better share.* This tradition has deep historical roots. When a warrior returned from a successful hunt he was expected to share some of the meat to his immediate family, friends, neighbors, and relatives. In times of famine the meat was stretched out as far as possible. Rare was the warrior who refused to fulfil this obligation because there were strict, implicit rules about sharing. Conversely, there were also taboos about not fulfilling this requirement reinforced by various means of disapproval ranging from humor to outright shunning.

At the time of first European contact there were many formalized institutional approaches to sharing among North American tribes such as the potlatch, which was practiced by West Coast Indians and the give-away dances sponsored by several plains tribes. Joe Dion describes a particular give-away dance among his people the Crees in which a woman experienced such joy and euphoria during a dance that she virtually gave everything away. Her husband was away from home at the time and he was somewhat chagrined on returning home to discover that even his horse and gun had been "danced away" (Dion, 1996: 52). Today several tribes still practice the give-away dance at special occasions designed to honor individuals.

Some historians point out that the traditional Indigenous practice of giving and taking was greatly affected by practices that arose at the time of first contact. As the fur trade got underway the First Nations were perceived as necessary allies in the enterprise and the fruits of their labors were a highly-valued commodity in the world market. Furs were traded for European-produced goods and gifts were exchanged as tokens of trust and goodwill. When the markets eventually dried up and the Indian economy was faced with the inevitable need to change, the perception of the First Nations was radically transformed. Suddenly the Indian became the "white man's burden," someone who needed to be taken care of and nothing to offer as a means of preserving integrity. There were even those who viewed the First Nations with the patronizing attitude of admiring "the noble savage" with the wish to preserve Aboriginal cultures for posterity (Friesen, 1995a: 24).

By the mid 1880s the buffalo were wiped out and neither government officials nor the First Nations were prepared for the rather sudden disappearance the latter's food supply. Government bureaucrats had envisaged that there would be an adjustment period during which the Indians gradually adapted to an agrarian model by planting and harvesting crops, and raising cattle. When these plans suddenly had to be modified the government simply concluded that they would temporarily help the First Nations out by giving them rations. The Indians, on the other hand, projecting a more traditional stance in keeping with their philosophy, concluded that the arrangement would become permanent. Their "grandfather" (another name for the Indian agent) would look after them. Besides, how could a self-respecting warrior conceive of gaining a livelihood by scratching the ground with a stick and then waiting for things to grow (Dempsey, 1991: 42). This background set the stage for a long-term dependency relationship that has lingered to this day. As a priest in Fort Chipewyan, Alberta, once remarked to one of the authors, "In the past we spent a lot of time teaching the Indians to receive. Initially, many of them were insulted by the process. Now, we wish to reverse the process and give them back their independence, and we are finding this a very difficult thing to do."

There is an element of a business-deal atmosphere to consider in this context which appears to have shifted to a dependency mode. Many Aboriginal leaders have interpreted treaty benefits on a broader basis than the written conditions indicated. They see government grants and rations as a form of regular and perpetual compensation for the elimination of the buffalo and for lands taken. For this reason Indian people are sometimes advised by their leaders not to feel any measure of shame or chagrin for receiving welfare monies or other forms of government subsistence. These are strictly to be viewed as honorable and appropriate compensation for ceded territories and the right of unlimited occupancy (Snow, 1977: 28f).

Traditional trading practices between First Nations and Europeans reflected mutual trust of sorts. Direct confrontation and negative exchanges were generally avoided. This perspective was deeply imbedded in Aboriginal culture whose leaders might have been viewed by outsiders as reluctant or hesitant. According to Cree elder Joseph Couture (1985: 9) Native people possess a kind of self-reliance which nonNatives often interpret as uncooperative, stubborn, belligerent, impossible or even "dumb." Indians also act with an aloofness which is easily perceived as a reluctance to ask for or receive help other than in an emergency or crisis. The fact is their live-and-let-live philosophy reflects an attitude of non-interference, for to interfere is to be discourteous, threatening, or even insulting. Although group goals are paramount and individual identity is primarily awarded through community channels, the Indigenous community reveals a very strong tendency to avoid any form of direct confrontation with the individual.

The inherent difficulty in trying to understand this aspect of Indian philosophy is imbedded in the European-inspired penchant for talking things out. The Native orientation is more inclined to stifle or repress issues or, if necessary, find a means by which to handle the matter by avoiding direct confrontation as much as possible. Feelings are not to be shown, especially grief and sorrow. These were traditionally seen as emotions which, if indulged, could threaten a group, for engagement in emotional states could incapacitate the person overwhelmed by them. Only when grief and sorrow were forgotten as quickly as possible could the group continue to meet survival challenges with the fullest attention and energy of every member (Ross, 1992: 29).

Even to this day when some measure of confrontation between Aboriginal individuals becomes necessary, it is often accomplished by telling a story or by relating a legend. In this context, the purpose of story-telling is simply a means by which to let the second party know that his or her behavior has been inappropriate. The hearer is then supposed to figure out that he/she is the target of the story and is expected to amend his/her ways. If the point of the story is missed or if the listener perceives its purpose to be other than informing, another means may be sought to amend the situation. Usually this kind of undertaking is not attempted more than once. Parenthetically, when it is attempted on the uninitiated nonNative individual the scene can have quite humorous side-effects. It is possible that nonNative listeners may become so engrossed in the story that they will make comments which clearly indicate their lack of awareness about what is transpiring. In one instance it did not occur to several individuals that they were the target of a particular story until one of them later related the incident to a third party. At that point the insight sparkled and the nonNative individual burst out, "Aha! This is about my behavior!"

In traditional Inuit society an indirect means of communication was in effect so that one spoke only of oneself in a form of the second person. An announcement that one was going hunting was spoken in this way, "Someone wants to go hunting," or "Someone is going to the sea." Other everyday plans and behaviors were conveyed in similar style, "Someone is hungry, someone is angry, someone is going to bed," and so on.

Respect for the individual in the Native community is often practiced to severe limits according to nonNative standards. For example, one woman removed her daughter from a particular school because the child, who was only seven years old, said she did not enjoy the school. After several days of absence the child was enrolled in another school. Similarly, when an Aboriginal truant officer visited a northern reserve home to determine why a ten-year-old was continually absent from school, the mother asked if the child was in school on the date of the visit. When the officer gave a negative response she simply replied, "Then I don't know. I *told* him!" The implicit belief is that if children are left to their own desires as much as possible, and not interfered with, they will develop both independence and a special loyalty to their parents.

persisted (Goulet, 2001). Still, there is justifiable concern that this may not be enough. Unless immediate steps are taken to maintain and strengthen the reservoir of Indigenous knowledge, it may be lost forever.

Battiste and Henderson (2000: 268) acknowledge three specific concerns about the diminishing status of Indigenous knowledge: (i) Aboriginal languages are not being maintained; (ii) First Nations children are spending much less time engaged in traditional activities on the land; and, (iii) Indian communities are increasingly relying on university-trained technicians for guidance in managing natural resources such as forestry and ecosystems. Although Battiste and Henderson do not appear ready to admit it, the reality is that the motivation to deal with these concerns will have to originate from within Aboriginal communities. No one cares as much about their knowledge as they do. Once the campaign to undertake this challenge is affirmed by the Aboriginal community, its urgency may be advanced in Canadian dominant society.

To be fair, the responsibility for maintaining Indigenous knowledge does not singly rest with Native people. The cultural and spiritual richness of Canada is affected by its possible erosion, to say nothing of the legal and moral responsibilities of government in this regard. Strong lobbying on the part of the First Nations could spur the government to fulfil its obligations. At this point, however, the going gets complicated. If governments are to take steps to ensure the strengthening of Indigenous cultural elements, how can Aboriginal people be certain that government programs will be commensurate with Aboriginal objectives? Based on past performance, it is a certainty that if government is involved, government influence (which represents the body politick) will be evident. Battiste and Henderson (2000: 270) encourage government intervention but recognize the possibility of cultural exploitation in the process. In their words:

> ... the most effective means of preventing the unjust exploitation of Indigenous peoples' knowledge is to ensure that the people have information, training, and institutional structures of their own by which to evaluate external research proposals, to negotiate collaborative agreements with outside researchers, and, if necessary, to take private legal action to prevent the licensing or sale of knowledge that is not properly acquired from them.

Battiste and Henderson's concerns are probably well-founded, but their appeal to government also raises complicated questions. If assisted by government, with all of its attending influences, how can the Aboriginal community be assured that they will be able to build or appropriate the right "information, training, and institutional structures" by which to "evaluate, negotiate, and engage in legal action?" Who will provide this information

Native people are not usually in the habit of providing extended answers such as those which exemplify nonNative explanations. Ask a nonNative why he or she was absent from an occasion at which they were expected to be present and an endless verbal harangue may result. Ask a Native person the same question and you may be rewarded with a one-word response or more likely, none at all. After all, if you respected the person, you would not even *ask* why they did not show up.

An AmerIndian leader observed recently that the Indigenous way relies heavily on effective early childhood education. Interpreted, this probably means that if Native children are given full opportunity to inculcate the old ways until they are six or seven years of age it will hardly ever be necessary to discipline them afterwards. This tradition has the advantage of encouraging children to become self-reliant and independent at a much earlier age than their nonNative counterparts. As such it is also a vital aspect of the philosophy of valuing and respecting individuality.

Most books about Indian ways mention that the traditional approach to child discipline, when it became necessary to implement it, was to avoid corporal punishment and instead to utilize humor, name-calling and ridicule as means of keeping individuals in line. In addition, the more informal means of social control were practiced by relatives or close friends, never by the parents. Doing so might jeopardize the bond between parent and child. In certain contexts today even nonNative people are expected to carry out these forms of discipline when necessary. If children become too boisterous, for example, and a nonNative person holds an accepted position such as a teacher, it will be expected that he or she will step in and bring order.

The ancient ways of sharing and caring will not readily be appreciated in a world increasingly highlighted by direct confrontation and self-assertiveness, but they do reflect a deep regard for one's peers. To some Canadians, the vulgar, abrasive, crude language used in so many media presentations are indicative of a society that has gone too far. A return to the old ways could be beneficial at this point, particularly if it also conveyed a more respectful attitude towards the rights of others.

(4) A Spiritual Sense of Community

All men were made by the same Great Spirit Chief. They are all brothers. The earth is the mother of all people, and all people should have equal rights upon it. – Chief Joseph, Nez Perce First Nation. (Friesen, 1998: 45)

> The great majority of nations have been formed, not by people who desired intensely to live together, but rather by people who would not live separately. – Jean-Charles Bonenfant, Quebec historian, The French Canadians and the Birth of Confederation. (Colombo, 1987: 84)

Many tribal societies traditionally believed themselves to have a special relationship with Deity, based partially on the grounds of tribal identity and longevity. Since the Creator had chosen them to dwell on this earth as a unique entity, obviously that meant something (Harrod, 1992: 38f). Many First Nations historically also gave themselves unique names signifying their special identity in the scheme of things. The Blackfoot (the preferred term in the United States is Blackfeet) peoples also believed they were a covenant people and they braided their hair as symbol of this link with the Creator. They were firm believers in the supernatural and, according to McClintock (1992: 167), they were subject to what were later called the Good and Evil forces that influence human affairs. Similarly, the Sioux believed that their Sacred Buffalo Calf Pipe, which had been handed down through the generations via procedures imbedded in the oral tradition, was the foundation of their religion. It too linked them with the supernatural. Lame Deer (Lame Deer and Erdoes, 1972: 128) once noted sarcastically, "You white men killed your Jesus; we Indians haven't killed our peace pipe yet."

Many North American First Nations have special inventories of sacred objects with long and unique histories. For them these objects form an incarnational connection with the Creator. The Potawatomi, for example, have their Sacred Chief Drum which was once presented to them as a symbol of a Divine link (Friesen, 1999: 208). The Cheyennes still value their Sacred Arrows, brought down to them from a Sacred Mountain in Wyoming called Devil's Tower (Looking Horse, 1988: 68), and the Sacred Buffalo Hat which was another symbol of Divine approval for their spirituality (Grinnell, 1976: 88). When the northern and southern Cheyenne divided into two camps around 1830, possibly because it was easier to manage affairs in smaller numbers, each division took one of the two sacred covenants with them. The northern group took the Sacred Buffalo Hat and the southern Cheyenne took the Sacred Medicine Arrows. Today the rite of renewal for the Sacred Medicine Arrows is an annual summer event during which the entire tribe is in a solemn mood. Originally the arrows were bestowed on the tribe by the Creator via the prophet, Sweet Medicine. In traditional times, it was believed that if the Sacred Arrows and the Sacred Hat were taken into battle, the tribe could not lose. Once, however, in 1830 a band of warring Pawnees stole the arrows and a long period of tribal catastrophe befell the Cheyennes. Now, once a year, shamans open the medicine bundle containing the Sacred Arrows in a solemn ritual. The arrows represent the collective existence of the Cheyenne Nation and in a sense they may be called the embodiment of the tribal soul (Hoebel, 1965: 7). The Sacred Buffalo Hat is perceived to be a living manifestation of supernatural power and represents a holy covenant which the Cheyenne have with the Creator. The Sacred Buffalo Hat was given to the nation by the prophet, Sacred Horns, at a sacred site in the north. In 1874 a tragedy befell the Sacred Hat when the keeper, Half Bear, died and his son, Coal Bear, was not present to receive the hat. When Coal Bear returned, the temporary keeper of the hat refused to give it up and thus the hat was spiritually contaminated. For a long time, as with the case of the loss of the Sacred Medicine Arrows, the tribe underwent many unfortunate happenings.

Belief in the importance of tribal identity downplays any notion of individuality as a separate entity. Any talents or gifts that an individual possesses must provide some benefit to the community or they are being misused. Any possession that individual may have must be available for use by any member of the community at any time. Traditionally, when there was a community need and someone had the means to fulfil that need, he or she would be expected to behave accordingly. If a vision quester was successful in his search, the blessings of his experience would be welcomed, validated and, hopefully, enhanced by and within the community. In the final analysis, it was the community, the people who mattered, not individual attainment.

There are definite benefits in valuing community above individuality. As Lowie points out in another context, in the "olden days" of Indian culture, an individual was always better off in the company of his peers.

> A man may be a champion marksman, but when there is no game to shoot he falls back on the pemmican his wife has stored against that very emergency; and even in the chase he is most efficient when he hunts in company. His robes and leggings are the work of his wives or kinsmen; his very arrows are not of his own making but of the handicraft of skilled craftsmen. If he seeks renown, what are his chances as a lonely raider? Even a well-organized party was likely to be cut to pieces or be hard put to it when fleeing from superior numbers. Crisis lowered on every side, and it meant everything to be able to face life not alone but with a comrade shielded by one's family and clan, in the bosom of one's club. (Lowie, 1956: 329)

Conclusion

Although the cultural inventories of the various First Nations revealed a measure of diversity at the time of European contact, there was some measure of universality among their ritualistic enactments and religious outlooks. Fortunately for scholars who have an appreciation for epistemological diver-

sity, many First Nations today still practice many aspects of their ancient tribal perspectives. They have clung tenaciously to these concepts despite the
many pressures to abandon their ways during the centuries following
European contact. Unlike many immigrant cultural groups they have resisted
the temptation to add the trappings of modern statehood and have continued
to revere their past. The Native cultural renaissance that began in the 1960s
has strengthened the will among First Nations to revive traditional customs
and bring them into the public domain. This motivation now affords
observers an excellent opportunity to study components of Aboriginal theology and related practice that were heretofore kept secret. This possibility also
allows interested observers to gain a deeper knowledge of First Nations' spirituality in a way that these insights can be compared with developing forms
of state religions such as Christianity. Whatever the outcome, we must be
grateful to the First Nations of North America for preserving so many of their
ancient cultural ways. There is no doubt that a study of them offers a form of
deep spiritual enrichment to the diligent observer.

A growing crescendo of Aboriginal voices has sounded in recent years to
emphasize the importance of a renewal of Indigenous knowledge and spirituality (Meili, 1992; Cajete, 1994; McGaa, 1995; Johnston, 1995; Bear
Heart, 1998; Weaver, 1998; Battiste, 2000b; Battiste and Henderson, 2000).
These writers have been accompanied by the voices of Indian elders in
attempting to explain Indigenous metaphysical systems. The good news is
that unlike a century or two ago, nonNatives are beginning to show interest
in what they have to say (Couture, 1991a).

Yazzie (2000) maintains that if the First Nations are to throw off the yoke
of epistemological colonialism, they must commence the process within
themselves. Political self-determination begins with internal sovereignty
which means taking control of one's personal, family, clan, and community
life. Essentially this means a return to tradition and a rejection of modern
EuroCanadian value systems. The latter will not be easy, as Findley (2000:
x) notes:

> The task of opposing the dominant orthodoxies of modernity from a
> position at their ever-extending margins, or from a strategically primi-
> tivist place outside, is crucial and dangerous work. . . . Significant num-
> bers of Euro-Canadian scholars have become remarkably good at cri-
> tiquing the pretensions and practices of modernity and defending mar-
> ginalized groups, but they do so within institutions among whose facul-
> ties Aboriginal people are minimally represented.

Battiste (2000b) insists that Aboriginal languages must be viewed as the
basic media for the transmission and survival of Indigenous knowledge. It is
Battiste's contention that unless the revival of Aboriginal languages becomes

a principal government undertaking, many of them will be lost along with the distinctive Aboriginal orientation to understanding the world from an holistic perspective. Unfortunately his improbable likelihood does not diminish the fact that the primary responsibility for maintaining Indigenous language and culture must be assumed by First Nations themselves. It cannot be safeguarded by government policies, school programs, or university degrees (Goulet, Dressyman-Lavallee, and McCleod, 2001: 45).

The maintenance of Indigenous languages must first of all be a demonstrated priority among First Nations themselves. They must know their languages in order to teach them. They must value them enough to put aside less important pursuits in the scheme of things and get on with the business of language teaching. This statement may not be welcomed by more politically-inclined Aboriginals, but it is reality.

Four

Traditional Aboriginal Pedagogy

Even a cursory survey of the traditional First Nations' world-view will confirm that their philosophy comprises a very unique metaphysical perspective (Medicine, 1987; Couture, 1991b). Like other ethnocultural communities, the Aboriginal people have always been concerned about passing on the truths they value to succeeding generations. At the time of first contact they had an elaborate method of transmitting valued knowledge in place which we know as the oral tradition. It is safe to say that the various First Nations even had fairly common methods of imparting instruction. Their belief system always premised on a deep underlying spiritual orientation that diffused physical, nonphysical, and personal elements into a connective unity.

Although the teaching methodologies of the various tribal configurations in North America featured a marked similarity, there were differences in skill emphasis. When a Huron mother needed to teach her daughters the art of farming and mothering, she emphasized different skills than the Blackfoot mother did who wanted her daughters to know how to clean and tan a buffalo hide. An Inuit man would be more concerned about his son's potential ice-fishing skills than his ability to build, launch, and guide a Nootka canoe. There is no doubt, however, that in all Indigenous populations the process of teaching/learning was somewhat formalized and began during the child's earliest days. Proper behavior patterns were instilled largely by indirect, non-coercive means (Miller, 1997: 18).

Methods of child discipline varied only slightly from one tribe to another. Usually stories with a moral were told to children who misbehaved and sometimes the youngsters were teased or made to feel embarrassed about their misdeeds. Miller (1997: 19) tells a Carrier story about four boys who humiliated an old woman and were punished by being relegated to a position in the sky as a constellation of stars. Ever after, when the people viewed these stars in the sky they reaffirmed this moral to their children, "Do not laugh at poor old people, but give them the driest log in your bundle."

The concept of apprenticeship was central to traditional Native education. Elders gifted with medicinal knowledge often selected apprentices to learn their skills and gain their knowledge. Those who held this knowledge let their proteges watch and learn and then participate in healing ceremonies in order for them to absorb and appreciate and later pass along this knowledge.

While scholars have explicated the parameters of these Aboriginal traditions from time to time, appreciation for their worth has not penetrated the pedagogical ranks of the contemporary teacher training milieu. This is unfortunate because an investigation of traditional Native pedagogy will reveal an inherent historical genius which has augured well for the maintenance of First Nations cultures through the centuries since first contact.

There are many illustrative historical accounts which substantiate the reliability of the Indigenous oral tradition. There are also many examples which show the written tradition to be found less than infallible. It is important to remember that the two traditions are not mutually exclusive, the written having grown out of the oral as a vital part of the natural progression of human civilization.

Defining the Oral Tradition

A common method of articulating the oral tradition is the intricately-devised deliberate process of verbally handing down stories, beliefs, and customs from one generation to the next. While this definition is technically correct, at the surface it glosses over the impact of the oral tradition when in certain circumstances it has the same effect as unwritten law. Among some plains tribes, when the tobacco was passed among a recognized group of elders it was understood that participants would be bound by the truth. Similarly, when a sweetgrass ceremony was enacted it indicated that a cleansing of the mind was the desire of the participants, and the way was prepared for honest and "pure" deliberation. Similarly, it was the purpose of the sweat-lodge ceremony to recoup spiritually; the outcome of the ceremony was determined by one's attitude on entering the sweat-lodge. If the individual's mind was clean, pure, and without malice, an inner cleansing and empowering could transpire. Participating in the ceremony without fulfilling this requirement could result in personal misfortune or affliction.

The oral tradition was not only a means by which to transmit cultural knowledge to succeeding generations, it was a way of preserving and interpreting truth for a specific time and place as well as for mediating elaborate ritualistic processes. This was not necessarily an uncomplicated procedure. By participating in ritualistic processes, powerful religious and moral sensibilities were evoked in the consciousness of the participants. Basic in this context were root symbolic forms which encoded the fundamental meanings borne in the oral tradition and enacted in the ritual processes (Harrod, 1992). The fact that the oral tradition did not feature written forms should in no way be construed to suggest that its structures were any less complex, nor its spiritual and moral impact any less significant than that expected and promulgated through a written form.

Dimensions of the Oral Tradition

The fundamental knowledge store which most plains tribes wanted to pass on to succeeding generations included truths related to origins and migrations, and maintenance of the traditional lifestyle. At the very basic level were verbal accounts explaining creation, many of which are in circulation today. The Assiniboines, for example, believe that Lake Winnipeg was the great water where Iktûmnî created the earth. The lake represents the centre of the world and they believe they were created there. One version of the Assiniboine creation legend goes like this.

> Iktûmnî (not to be confused with the Creator), made the waters and the land. He also made heaven as well as day and night. After he made all the universe he created fourteen humans, but he did not want them to multiply immediately until they found a good dwelling place. He then selected seven fowl and ordered them to dive into the bottom of the sea and bring up some mud. The birds were unsuccessful and soon floated to the surface dead. Iktûmnî then sent down the muskrat, the mink, the beaver, and the fisher, but they too were unsuccessful. They too died in their attempt to bring up mud. However, Iktûmnî found a little mud in the claws of one of the deceased animals and used it to create the earth. Then he added some lakes for a water source.

> Iktûmnî taught the people everything they needed to know in order to survive on the earth and told them to multiply and prosper. The fourteen people were divided into seven couples and in time they became the ancestors of the Seven Council Fires of the North American Indians. (Healy, 1983: 1-2)

A cursory analysis of the story reveals a number of significant truths to be appropriated by the listeners. The Assiniboine Nations saw themselves specially made by Iktûmnî. The tribe was created in a special place and for a special purpose. The creation process constituted a medium of Divine caring for the Assiniboines. The selection of the various forms of wildlife in the creation process underscored the importance of several different numbers including the sacred number four.

Another origin story emanates from the Tsuu T'ina (Sarcee) Nation in Alberta who originated from the Beaver First Nation further north. As a result both the Beavers and the Tsuu T'ina have their own versions of how this transpired. The Tsuu T'ina interpretation suggests that the original division occurred many years ago in midwinter when the Beavers were crossing a frozen lake stretching east and west. When the people reached the middle of the lake a older woman noticed an animal horn protruding from the ice. Out of curiosity, she pulled on the horn, the ice trembled and groaned, then broke open in a wide crack. Half of the tribe was left on either side of the crack and both groups fled the scene out of fear. Those on the north side returned home to their historic hunting grounds while the southern group kept going until they reached their present locale. They henceforth became known as the Tsuu T'ina First Nation (Dempsey, 1978).

Structure of the Oral Tradition

The content and institutional structures of the oral tradition historically relied on several basic motifs. Among the Blackfoot, Crows, Cheyennes, and Arapahos, for example, four specific motifs were used – solar, astral, animals, and plants. In the first two types, the heavenly bodies played a significant role, particularly as sources of transcendental power. Animals often mediated powers to humans that were associated with their unique characteristics – speed, vision, wisdom, or cunning. They also employed in adventuresome and comic tales related for entertainment purposes (Underhill, 1965). Plants played a less dominant role, albeit among the Crows, for example, the cultivation of tobacco was connected to their origin story. For them the ritual of the Tobacco Society is a reenactment of the creation story which renews the people and their world (Harrod, 1992). Consider the following summary of their creation story.

> One day Old Man Coyote was staring across the vast waters and he suddenly felt very lonely. As he scanned the waters he saw two red-eyed male ducks paddling towards him. As they approached he enquired of them as to whether or not they had seen any other living beings. They gave a negative reply so Old Man Coyote got an idea.
>
> "You both swim and dive," he said. "Why don't you dive down into the waters and see what you can find?"
>
> The ducks obliged. One of them stayed with Coyote and the other did as was suggested. After some time had lapsed the diving duck appeared with something in his mouth. To Coyote it looked like a tree branch or

root. He then asked the duck to dive down a second time and the bird obliged, this time he came up with mud in his beak.

"Now that is something we can use," Coyote observed enthusiastically. He then fashioned an island from the mud. The ducks were excited at Coyote's manoeuvres and one of them exclaimed.

"Wouldn't it be nice if the island were not so bare?" Coyote then took the root that the duck had brought up and made trees, grass, and other plants from it. Now the island looked good. As the three of them were admiring the island, Coyote decided it would look even more beautiful if he added rivers, and valleys, and canyons.

Now the ducks glowed with pleasure, but Coyote was still not satisfied. "I am lonely," he said. "I need company, someone I can talk to." Then he took some mud and made men. Then he made women for the men, to be companions for them.

"Can you make companions for us too," the ducks asked. So Coyote made some female ducks for them. Now, finally, the earth was beautiful and everyone was happy. (Hoxie, 1989: 13-15)

Emergence of Written Forms

Traditionally the oral tradition was well-suited to a fairly conservative human tradition that was given only occasionally to and relatively minor shifts. No human civilization can function without some element of change, however, and the oral tradition was appropriately flexible to accommodate this societal need. By contrast, when the written tradition emerged, and then enhanced with the invention of the printing press, it lent an element of false security to human civilization. The printed page was immediately viewed as constituting a "provable" record, even a legal foundation by which to affect future developments. Now it was possible to refer to recordings of past happenings without having to consult the elders; history in this sense, "spoke for itself."

As an aside it is useful to keep in mind that while this view is somewhat overstated, so is the belief that the written record is free from interpretations geared to time and place. In addition, the printed page has produced some unforeseen side-effects, not all of them necessarily positive. House (1992), for example, contends that the printed page beget nationalism in the capacity that written forms of propaganda influenced people to perceive of themselves as belonging to an entity beyond specific geographic limitations. By reading about their broader identity, they could feel part of something more expansive than their local tribe. They could even be stirred to die for their larger ethnocultural community or nation without even experiencing face-to-face contact with other members of their wider fraternity (Friesen, 1993: 67).

The Utility of Legends

Traditionally, one of the primary avenues by which children were educated among First Nations was through the use of legends. Legend telling, however, was supplemented by other established institutional practices such as rituals, ceremonies, and symbols. The stories were very old, passed on from one generation to the next through the use of traditional language emphasizing valued concepts (Knockwood and Thomas, 1994: 15). The storytellers, usually grandparents or elders, emphasized living harmoniously with creatures of the land, sea, and air or, as the Sioux would say, "all our relations." Even plants were said to have spirits and were regarded as relations and like all living phenomena, were potential teachers.

Legends dealt with spirituality, the origins of things, the performances of medicine men and medicine women, and the bravery and singleheartedness of warriors (Ewers, 1989; Grinnell, 1962). They conveyed a vast range of cultural knowledge including folkways, values, and beliefs including the fundamental metaphysical presuppositions that determine the very ground of a particular cultural pattern. As a primary construct of the oral tradition, the telling of Indian legends constituted a vast cultural storehouse and served as a primary tool for cultural maintenance and tribal history. Even today legends may be considered a major part of Aboriginal oral literature and each form is somewhat unique to the particular tribal cultural configuration to which it belongs. Indian stories are pictures of Indian life drawn by Indian artists, showing life from their point of view.

It should be noted that although relating legends was a mainstay of eldership, not all elders were recognized storytellers. In fact, in many First Nations there were distinctions about elder functions. Some elders were blessed with knowing tribal secrets in the form of stories, rituals, ceremonies, and Indigenous knowledge. They shared their knowledge when it was time to do so with selected audiences, starting with young children. Later on they would elaborate the more intricate details of their knowledge with hand-picked young men and women who were to be entrusted with the responsibility of passing on the sacred knowledge. The elders recognized that education of the young was concerned with character formation, the making of human beings. As Akan (1992: 194) states:

> Children who do not yet have a good sense of morality are believed to
> be incomplete human beings. To be wholly human means to have a good

sense of right and wrong and be able to act on that knowledge. For a traditional Saulteaux teacher and parent, this carries a tremendous responsibility because it means giving the children a good spirit.

Although their roles are not as clearly specified today, traditionally there
were elders who had recognized gifts pertaining to medicinal knowledge and
they were approached when someone fell ill. There were also elders who possessed skills in counselling; they were sought out if an individual had a problem to discuss, or planned to get married, or needed a dream or vision interpreted. Wisdom elders were also sought out by band councils when major
decisions had to be made involving the entire community. Elders were generally regarded as human storehouses of valued knowledge, skills, and wisdom. They knew about the seasonal cycles of edible and medicinal plants,
and the relocation habits of migrating birds, animals and fish. They knew
about weather patterns, and they knew which hunting and trapping methods
worked best in regard to whatever prey was being sought.

Legend Typology

The study of Indian legends can be a source of enriched learning, illustrative of the sophistication of pre-Colonial First Nations education.
Traditionally, legends were told for a variety of purposes and in at least two
specific settings, formal and informal. The latter often took place at the spur
of the moment when it appeared appropriate to entertain or perhaps to repri-
mand someone. Also, sometimes on a winter evening when the people had
stretched out to rest for the night a storyteller would begin a tale. Clark
(1988) suggests that it was good to tell stories in the winter because the
nights were so long. Some tribes feared telling stories in the summer because
the animals and birds, the chief characters in the stories, would hear people
talking and might be offended by what they heard.

Among Crow storytellers, on a long winter's night, a narrator might
expect to get an occasional response from this listeners, failing which he
assumed that they had fallen asleep and he would stop talking (Lowie, 1963).
Unlike casual storytelling, the more formal aspect of the art was preserved
for deliberate moral or spiritual instruction. Some legends or myths were so
sacred as to have their telling restricted to the celebration of an event such as
the sundance. On such occasions, only recognized or designated persons
could engage in their telling.

In analyzing the composition of Indian legends it is possible to identify
at least *four* types specifically in operation among plains tribes. Although the
legends may be differentiated for the purpose of analysis, there was also con-

siderable overlap in their structure and use. The major types include: (i) *entertainment legends,* which were often about the Trickster (sometimes called Napi, Coyote, or Iktûmnî), and related primarily for the purpose of amusement; (ii) *teaching legends,* which were employed for the purpose of dispensing information about natural phenomena or tribal beliefs and customs; (iii) *moral legends,* which were intended to suggest to the hearer that a certain behavior should be enacted; and, (iv) *spiritual legends,* which could be related only by an Elder or other approved individual at a designated time and place.

On examination it will become evident that the *first* type of legends, entertainment legends are often highly amusing even to nonIndian listeners. The primary character is often the Trickster, a sort of half-human, half-god-like character with supernatural powers which he can use at will. John Snow (1977: 10), former Chief of the Wesley Band of the Stoney (Nakoda Sioux) First Nations has referenced the story of Iktûmnî and the fox.

> One day Iktûmnî finds a nest of duck eggs by a lakeshore and decides to make a meal of them. Carefully he makes a fire, cooks the eggs, then goes for a walk before partaking of his meal. As he walks around the lake, he meets a fox who appears to be limping. Grinning wickedly, Iktûmnî challenges the fox to a foot race around the lake to where his cooked eggs are waiting. He teases the fox by telling him about the waiting meal, convinced that he can easily outrun the wounded animal.

> Surprisingly, the fox agrees to the race and suggests that he will run around the treed side of the lake which Iktûmnî knows is actually the long way around. The Trickster quickly agrees and takes off at an easy pace. As soon as he is out of sight, the fox abandons his faked injury and races off to eat the eggs. When he is finished, he puts the shells into formation so they look as though they are ready to eat. When Iktûmnî arrives he assumes that the poor fox has not yet made it around the lake. "Poor dumb fox," he chortles, then sits down to eat. He quickly discovers that empty shells are all that's left of his anticipated banquet. Now he knows he has been taken in by the clever fox.

> Naturally, Iktûmnî is very angry, but there is nothing he can do. The fox is long gone. "Just wait till I see that fox again," he mutters, and goes off to his next adventure.

Trickster stories often involve playing tricks, that is, the Trickster plays tricks on others and they play tricks on him. The Trickster has an advantage on his unsuspecting audience, however, since he can deploy his special powers on a whim to startle or to shock. He has the capacity to raise animals to life and he may even die now and then, but in four days he always comes to life again. In the Assiniboine story of the Trickster and the bear, the Trickster deceives the bear into thinking that if he enters a sweat lodge which the Trickster has built the bear will improve his vision. Once lured inside the Trickster proceeds to kill the bear and then prepares to cook the meat. He orders two birds to get him a proper cooking utensil (which takes the birds four tries and provides an interesting diversion), and then gathers the animals of the forest together for a feast.

During the festivities the Trickster has an argument with the rock on which he is sitting about the choice of desired meat cuts. The Trickster wants the head of the bear but so does the rock. The rock then decides to stick itself onto Trickster's bottom who then cannot move. When the animals discover this they run off with all the bear meat. Trickster is finally jarred from the rock by two hard-flying birds who on his order bump him from his station – on their fourth try, of course. He then sets out to retrieve his meat. He is about to give up when he discovers an otter sitting in a tree branch eating bear meat. When the Trickster orders the otter to drop some meat into his open mouth beneath the branch, the otter agrees to this, but asks the Trickster to close his eyes. When he wearies of the chore of feeding the Trickster, the otter drops a sliver of wood into the Trickster's mouth who promptly chokes and dies. On the fourth day he comes back to life and continues his adventures by travelling in a different direction.

When this legend is told the individual storyteller may embellish certain scenes according to whim. Aside from being amusing the story incorporates several principal aspects of Plains Indian culture – the bear, the sweat-lodge, the relationship between the Trickster and animals, and reference to the sacred number four. In this sense the story could also be delineated as instructional, or at least confirming of certain cultural components.

The *second* type of legend, teaching legends, often utilize animal motifs to explain why things are the way they are. For example, the Nakoda child may enquire about the origins of the seasons and another Trickster story may ensue. Among the Nakoda Sioux of northwest Canada, the account of how winter originated may go something like this. One day the animals got together with the Trickster to decide what the season should be like and how long it should last. The beaver suggests that the length of winter in terms of months of duration be determined by the number of scales on his flat tail. The animals consider this to be excessive, but since there is no voiced alternative, the suggestion is taken. The result is that the winter lasts so long that most of the animals barely survived. The poor squirrel ends up crying so hard that he develops white marks around his swollen eyes which remain to this day. Thus another meeting is called and this time the rabbits suggest a shorter winter season. The frog demurs, insisting on a six-month winter. The other animals disagree and one of them slaps the frog so hard he falls into the nearby pond. He thrives in that location to this day. Then, after another lengthy discussion the frog's suggestion is taken and the six-month length of Canadian winter is established.

The origin of winter story again incorporates familiar elements of First Nations' cultural lore, namely, that living creatures have a role to play in the ongoings of the universe. Parenthetically, we learn why the squirrel's eyes appear the way they do, and why frogs live in ponds, clearly side-benefits of the legend. In addition the story confirms the length of the winter and thereby comprises a means of explanation, particularly to youthful listeners, why things are the way they are.

The Micmac story explaining the nature of the loon's call involves Glooscap about whom many such stories are related. It seems Glooscap gives loon a unique call, quite different than the other creatures. Loon is a deep diving bird, but one day he overdoes it and gets caught on the weeds at the bottom of a lake. When the loon calls for help, Glooscap knows immediately who is beckoning him and he dives down to help. Then he restricts the loon to shallow diving only, which henceforth explains that particular behavior pattern on the part of the loon (Norman, 1990).

The *third* type of legend, moral legends, comprise a more complex configuration of functioning than both entertainment and instructional legends. These stories were traditionally related in formal settings only by individuals approved as storytellers. The subject matter of these tales is much more impending as, for example, the story of the blind man and the loon. The story varies among plains tribes with the central character being of either sex. In the Stoney version, the legend is based on a man and wife who are separated from their people when their tribe relocates. The man is blind and cannot hunt for himself. His wife does not love him. Still, she finds a buffalo for him to shoot, helps the man point his bow and arrow at the animal, and he fires a successful shot killing the buffalo. The wife informs him that his shot missed, then she takes their child and abandons her husband to secretly cut up and dry the meat for herself. In the meantime the blind man consults with the loon who tells the man to dive deeply into a nearby lake four times and his sight will be restored. The man does as he is told and his sight is restored on the fourth dive. As a payment for his advice the loon requests that the man then find his wife and cut off her breasts and bring them to the loon. The man complies with the command and then rewards the loon with a claw necklace which the loon wears to this day.

The lesson implied in the legend is obviously that selfishness and lying to one's mate are punishable forms of behavior. Parenthetically, the legend also informs the audience about the origins of the loon's necklace. In a Dogrib version of the story the loon requests that the man kill his wife, and in a West Coast version the story concerns a blind old man and a wicked old crone. A Tsuu T'ina version posits the setting of a blind medicine man and his wife, with the latter not convinced of the merits of her mate's wisdom. Starvation besets the tribe, and hungry, dangerous wolves skulk surround the camp looking for food. The medicine man appears helpless and ill-equipped to advise on how to rectify the situation. Finally, the blind medicine man calls on his guardian spirit, the loon, and then tells his wife to show him where to aim his bow and arrow toward the enemy wolves. She does so and he shoots the biggest wolf thus providing food for the camp. The medicine man's powers are restored and he thanks the loon with a claw necklace.

According to some contemporary Aboriginal elders, it is not appropriate to propagate Indian legends containing violent scenes or brutality to uninitiated audiences. It is feared that outsiders might misjudge the intent of the legends and misunderstand or make erroneous assumptions regarding Aboriginal traditions. Traditional legends sometimes do incorporate cruel or violent behaviors, for example, the Stoney version of the loon story which involves cutting off the woman's breasts as punishment for her misbehavior to her husband. NonNatives may regard this scene as standard fare in Aboriginal storytelling without appreciating the content of the tradition. They may conclude that this kind of cruelty was an acceptable form of punishment for disrespectful mates in First Nations societies. One way out of the dilemma is to be reminded that almost every culture has an element of unorthodoxy in its folklore, for example, Bible stories, Aesop's fables, and Grimm's fairy tales, all quite matter-of-factly incorporate accounts of people being put to death. Why pick on the Indian folklore? Parallel with elders' concern it is interesting to point out that the "legends" of modern times as seen on prime time television every night of the week may be interpreted by succeeding generations as illustrative of a very violent culture.

The *fourth* type of legend may described as a spiritually-impacting story, but it would be inappropriate to discuss such tales in this context because the accounts are considered the personal possessions of certain respected individuals. Respecting this preference on the part of First Nations is a recent perspective, probably indicative of a growing sensitivity toward and appreciation for the ways of the Indigenous People. Decades ago, spiritual stories were recorded and published by anthropologists, for example, the well-know Blackfoot Lodge Tales (Grinnell, 1962), but this practice has since ceased. In respect of this perspective no spiritual legend will be related nor summarized here.

Several years ago it was our privilege to work with a team of Stoney educators on a legend-publishing project. At the outset it was made clear to the team by tribal elders that members of the project group were not qualified to

deal with sacred or spiritual legends. Some elders even questioned the concept of publishing legends in the first place though the intent of the project
was to provide published materials as requested local school curricula. It was
explained to the elders that the project team saw their role only as that of pro-
curers and translators. They did not perceive their mandate in any sense as
editors or "explainers." The project group promised not to change the intent
or meaning of any of the legends which they recorded as related to them by
elders. In the oral tradition, of course, changes in story form occurred during
the telling though this privilege was allotted only to recognized storytellers.
In this project that time-honored tradition was held in abeyance since the
process was to record and print, not to tell legends. Added to this was the
importance of recognizing that probing into the content of spiritual legends
is a very delicate activity. After all, many legends represent the arena of
sacred teachings among the tribes. This fact required that the various dimensions of the project be conducted with appropriate respect.

In one southwest tribe the relating of spiritual legends required very
elaborate procedures. The services of the elder had to be requested four days
before the scheduled delivery and "payment" (gift giving) for the telling
arranged. The elder prepared for the event by fasting and offering tobacco.
Further, there was a designated time for telling sacred legends and during
four specific four days during the winter solstice, "when the sun stands still,"
no payment was required. Relating a scared legend could be arranged on
other winter nights but payment was required. Under no circumstances, however, could the sacred legend, nor any part of it be told in the summer
(Underhill, 1965).

Parameters of Legend-Telling

The cultural repertoire of every traditional North American First Nation
has legends about the origins of things (Knudtson and Suzuki, 1992). Their
religious systems have evolved from their basic beliefs about the universe
and most such systems were so historically remarkably elaborate and complex that it was beyond the power of their participants to explain them fully
to outsiders who, in turn, lacked the necessary sense of appreciation (that is
the culturally-innate "urge to know"), that was required to comprehend what
was being related. Traditionally, origin legends were not told related to just
anyone who asked. In many tribes the property aspect of origin stories carefully safeguarded their maintenance. Selected individuals would learn a legend by careful listening; then, on mastering the story, would pass it on to a
member or members of the next generation, perhaps slightly changing
aspects of the story to suit their own moods, experiences or perceptions. The

amendments might centre on a different choice of animals or sites referred to in the story preferred by the teller.

A tribe's origin belief or myth was central to the entire religious system of most traditional First Nations, and often based on these assumptions: (i) everything in the universe, including people, has spiritual power, or life force; (ii) all spiritual forces are interconnected; and, (iii) mankind has a responsibility to that interconnection. The earth, which is the basis for such connections and which provides life to all is sacred (Josephy, 1989). Thus sacred legend-telling comprises instruction in spiritual education at its most significant level.

Telling entertainment legends was usually a public venture, for these stories might be related by almost anyone at any time. Since Aboriginal tribes rarely corporally punished their children they often found it useful to hint at the inappropriateness of undesirable behavior by telling somewhat ridiculous stories of some animal which engaged in some such act, hoping that the child would catch on that their misbehavior was the object of the telling (Underhill, 1965). In this sense entertainment legends also became instructional.

Legend Supplements

Legends comprised only a part of a tribe's spiritual system which also included ceremonies, rituals, festivals, songs, and dances. These cultural attachments often involved physical objects such as fetishes, pipes, painted designs, medicine bundles, and sacred places. Familiarity with these components comprised religious knowledge, and everything learned was committed to memory. Viewed together, these entries represented spiritual connections between people and universe which, with appropriate care, resulted in a lifestyle of assured food supply, physical well-being, and the satisfying of the needs and wants of the society and its members (Josephy, 1989).

The structure of Indian legends follow an entirely different format and procedure than similar stories in EuroCanadian culture. There is a great deal of overlap among legends of varying plains tribes, for example, but often two versions of the same story in the same tribe might have only the same beginning in common. Then each version would digress. The stories could be told in almost identical language for a few paragraphs and then be changed to suit the narrator. The digression is designed to accommodate the style of the narrators who are at liberty to incorporate their personal everyday experiences in the telling. Fundamentally, however, legends primarily constitute the fluid aspect of pedagogical accompaniment to more deeply-entrenched institutional forms of traditional Native society. Hence, their utility has always been viewed as more functional because of a long-standing tradition of allowing a greater degree of flexibility in form than their parallel, more structural cultural counterparts.

The Implications of Process

With the announcement of a Canadian multicultural policy nearly three decades ago, interest in cultural nuances on the part of the various national ethnocultural communities has surged (Comeau and Driedger, 1978; Anderson and Frideres, 1981). Parallel with this development is a renewed interest in First Nations history and culture which may also spawn new understandings of and appreciation for cultural diversity. But here any similarity to other ethnocultural groups ends because the situation of the Aboriginal peoples in Canada is in many ways quite different from that of either Canada's Charter nations of Canada or the more recently-arrived immigrants, though the latter have opted for many of the same maintenance techniques.

Historically, Aboriginal peoples possess the right of first occupancy. Geographically, they have always occupied a different continent from that of the newcomers (First Nations have always been occupants of North America), who have manufactured the nation's multicultural policies. Culturally, the Indigenous people have maintained a unique philosophical stance, namely that of respecting the balance of nature, with technological advance being assigned a subordinate or corollary status. In economic terms, the First Nations now occupy the lower levels of income groups in Canada, which has made it difficult for them to wield a significant power base. Legally, they are the object of special laws which identify them as a separate group and set them apart from the larger society (Berry, 1981). Though these unique characteristics set the Native peoples apart in significant ways, the reality of the need for employing workable cultural maintenance techniques connects them indubitably with their fellow Canadians. How the successful transition from the oral tradition to more technologically-influenced methodologies will eventually come about will need to be initiated by First Nations. It is they who understand their traditions best though the struggle to have those ways understood and appreciated is probably still a long way off. Like most everything else, their preferred format for the teaching/learning process is still perceived by nonNatives in European-influenced ways.

Adherence to the oral tradition implies an entirely unique set of parameters by which to evaluate pedagogical procedures. At first glance the differences between oral and written forms of communication appear evident, but a more intense examination reveals a series of more subtle, far-reaching differences. Small wonder that these differences were not appreciated by the first explorers, fur traders, and missionaries. Nevertheless the potential benefits to be gained from contrasting the two approaches, with a view to gaining possible reciprocal advantage appear promising. This approach may even have implications for the improvement of contemporary pedagogical approaches. Perhaps now, with the First Nations cultural renaissance fully underway, nonNative educators will be prepared to listen and learn (Friesen, 1997). The possible learning opportunities may be sketched in three specific ways.

In the *first* instance, it must be underscored that the knowledge content of the traditional First Nations philosophy and lifestyle, which has quite consistently been successfully passed on to succeeding generations, must be viewed as a whole. It is viewed as comprising a series of interconnections. There is no perceived break in the line of development of "truth" through time; there is no segregation of essence, that is, no difference is noted between material and metaphysical qualities; and there is no breakdown of any kind between sacred and secular realms. This contrasts dramatically with any contemporary breakdown of "truth" which implies that only the secular domain is a rightful object of state-sponsored pedagogical scrutiny.

Traditional Native education reflected "all of life," that is, every element of their cultural lifestyle was incorporated into the teaching and learning process. Curricular motifs were drawn from everyday encounters with the creature world that supplied all of the tribe's needs. Legends, which were a primary vehicle of transmission, incorporated a wide range of teaching objectives – instructional, moral and spiritual, with a whole series of intertwined lessons to be learned during the relating of any particular tale. Unless our current perspective of legitimate knowledge spheres is expanded to include the spiritual domain, we shall have yet another case of "never the twain shall meet."

A *second* component of traditional Indian pedagogy was its emphasis on societal change and individuality. The curriculum, in the form of rituals, celebrations, and legends, changed as tribal customs were amended in response to impending circumstances. These changes were subsequently anticipated and modified by individual enactments and in relating cherished legends. The recognition of possession pertaining to such sacred items as legends, medicine bundles, pipes, painted tepee designs, etc., assured a certain established form of protection for the curriculum in so far as these were the property of elders alone. They alone, having been awarded the privilege of tribal trust through an unspoken but formal method of selection, held in their hands the metaphysical comprehensions of the tribal destiny of their people.

Though not unaffected by change, this office guaranteed a stability to the tribe and to the various operations necessary for its survival. By contrast, our contemporary ever-changing society has little patience for stability. New modes of styles, habits, "media truths" and ways of thinking are constantly being sought.

A *third* factor has to do with the subject of evaluating performance. In the classroom of the First Nations student, evaluation was traditionally a matter of personal accountability between teacher and pupil. Student performance was judged by the instructor who might in one instance be a storyteller and in another the primary actor in an elaborate ritual. Subsequent enactments by students would indicate their degree of readiness for possible leadership in the community. By the same token, student performance would reflect the teacher's ability to teach. No one could refer to achievement on any form of standardized test because evaluation was based on actual performance. An elder might be consulted about possible tribal relocation, the feasibility of a hunt or advice concerning enemy confrontation, and the "proof was in the pudding." If the advice was sound, the results inevitably would benefit the tribe. Conversely, if the advice proved to be inappropriate, certain measures could be taken, not necessarily on an immediate basis, but they could ultimately result in as drastic an action as a portion of the tribe breaking away from the main body to form a new band.

For the First Nations student in pre-colonial times, a successful educational experience implied commitment to a lifetime of learning, perhaps eventually translating individual talents to a specific teaching mode. If the stamp of approval was awarded by the tribe, the individual might be assigned an enhanced measure of responsibility or awarded a specific honor. As Chief John Snow of the Stoney Nation put it, "When a revelation becomes open to you, you will become a special person to our tribe" (Snow, 1977:12). Contemporary educators could learn from this. A great deal of time is spent in educational circles today extolling the virtues of individualized learning, yet we continually find convenient excuses (like inadequate financing), to explain why this virtuous objective cannot be attained.

The efficacy of the unique philosophical orientation of the First Nations has been vindicated through time as their beliefs, customs, and traditions have prevailed against the onslaught of a European-inspired cultural campaign to wipe out their very existence. With the passing of time this resistance has strengthened to become a bulwark of renaissance of traditional Indian ways (Cardinal, 1977; Lincoln, 1985). Perhaps, as the campaign picks up speed, nonIndian observers will take the opportunity to benefit from this very old and unique perspective. Not the least of areas to be affected by this sharing of ideas might be the arena of effective teaching.

Today there is a resurgence of interest in the old ways and elders are again being called upon to teach the young. Battiste and Henderson (2000: 87) demand recognition of the fact that Indigenous people have the right to exercise and transmit their own knowledge and heritage as legitimate subject matter. They also emphasize that both Native and nonNative worlds can derive great benefits from this knowledge and heritage. The old ways can build self-esteem for Native youngsters and widen the horizons of EuroCanadian thinking. Witt (1998: 270) cautions that any program targeted at enhancing individual self-esteem through language and culture programs must be founded within the stronghold of that culture. Basing a healing and self-esteem agenda on a different cultural process is like saying that Native culture and spirituality are not valid. By the same token, merely adding Native components to the content of an altogether nonNative curriculum will only increase acculturative stress on students.

Many Aboriginal elders believe that language is the key to learning traditional knowledge. Kirkness (1998a) insists that the majority of Aboriginal people in Canada are adamant that Native languages must be protected, preserved, promoted, and practiced in daily life. Fettes and Norton (2000) insist that the federal government establish a program for Aboriginal languages within the Department of Canadian Heritage instead of funding piecemeal incentives. They suggest the that latter be replaced by provincial and territorial funding agreements. This is not likely to happen unless the EuroCanadian body politick who elect governments begin to understand and affirm the value of Indigenous language and knowledge. That will only happen when First Nations themselves become agents of cultural transmission and begin to integrate the richness of their cultural repertoire into the Canadian mainstream.

There is also good news. Today, teaching elders are beginning to combine the cultural lessons they offer to the young with language learning. Native youngsters are taught about their heritage in traditional ways – through story-telling, modelling, and on-the-job training. A first thrust is for them to become aware of the historical process inflicted by the EuroCanadian education system on various generations of Aboriginal people. This awareness can assist in the development of a positive self-identity. Because education is a primary socializing agent in the community, one of its main goals needs to be the development of programs that will promote positive self-identity for students (Antone, 2000). When this is attained, it may be possible to gain a healthy appreciation for the old ways.

As the Indigenous peoples struggle to regain some semblance of relevance in the educational experiences of their young, it may be stated with some degree of confidence that some progress has been made in Native education over the past few decades. Improvements include better facilities, local control of schooling, counselling services and support groups. In many cases Native teachers have been trained to work in their own communities, and school curricula have been revised to include more culturally relevant content. As Tsuji (2000) cautions, other important considerations should also be noted. In addition to being concerned about what is to be taught, educators should be alert to *when* something should be taught. This variable is important to any educational program that stresses cultural relevance as the what and how factors. Other items to factor in include the realization that learning occurs throughout the year, not only when school is in session. Learning does not only occur in the confines of the school year; it happens at home, in the bush, on the trapline or during a hunt. All human experiences must be considered as having learning potential.

The bottom line for Native education is that is must be tailored to fit Aboriginal needs. If Native education is to have an identity of its own, then its formulators must make a conscious decision as to whether or not to mimic nonNative models. Otherwise they will simply find themselves targeting and realizing nonNative values, lifestyles, philosophies, and outcomes (Marker, 2000).

There is also good news on the post-secondary front. Although the tendency for Native students to pursue post-secondary education is of fairly recent origins, progress is being made. Aboriginal students only began to attend post-secondary institutions in any significant numbers during the 1970s. By 1981, the Canadian census revealed that two percent of the Aboriginal population held university degrees, compared with 8.1 percent of the nonAboriginal population. By 1990 the percentage of Native people holding university degrees rose to 2.6 percent compared with 12.6 for the nonNative population. When the Royal Commission of Aboriginal People appeared in 1996, it indicated that 4.2 percent of Aboriginal people held university degrees compared with 15.5 percent of nonAboriginals. Data shows that 21 percent of Aboriginals had completed a college certificate compared with 25.5 percent of nonAboriginals. In the following years these statistics kept rising; the number of Status Indians and Inuit enrolled in postsecondary institutions almost doubled between 1988/89 and 1997/98, rising from 15 572 to 27 100.

What is needed now is assurance from Indigenous elders that university educated Aboriginal youth will be sufficiently acquainted with First Nations' ways to be able to integrate that knowledge into the Canadian mainstream.

Five

The Evolution of Aboriginal Education in Canada

Although North American First Nations had a proficient means of transmitting valued knowledge and skills in place when the Europeans arrived, the latter did not take time to learn about it. Instead, their ethnocentric bent quickly led them to conclude that the Indigenous peoples were in dire need of a European-style civilization. The means by which they hoped to accomplish this goal was via instruction in schools designed by European architects of learning combined with heavy doses of religion.

Canadian Explorations

French exploration of the St. Lawrence Valley began in 1534 with the three voyages of Jean Cartier, followed by Samuel de Champlain in 1608. Although the first newcomers to the land that later became Canada were primarily explorers, they were quickly followed by individuals who had a religious purpose in mind.

The first missionaries who followed Cartier were a reform branch of Franciscans called Récollects who worked among the Hurons in New France as early as 1615. The Capauchins devoted themselves to educating the Micmac in Acadia as early as 1632, but their methods were quite unorthodox when viewed in today's light. The slave labor systems which these priests operated between the years 1690 and 1845 were a forerunner of the boarding school concept of imprisonment. The construction of mission stations was accomplished by Indigenous peoples who were allowed to occupy a living space measuring seven feet by two feet sometimes described as "specially-constructed cattle pens" (Churchill, 1998: 141). The Aboriginals were forced to live in deplorable conditions, working hard to construct elaborate religious edifices while living on diets of less than 1 400 calories per day. An open pit served as a toilet facility for literally hundreds of people.

The first legislation passed by the British Parliament concerning Aboriginal people occurred in 1670 and was quite unspecific in intent. The implicit message of the policy was that the government would look after or protect the Indians, principally because they were useful to the fur trade. A dramatic shift in policy occurred in 1830 when the fur trade waned and the government viewed First Nations from a different perspective. Almost overnight the mood shifted and Indian people were suddenly depicted as living in a state of "barbarism and savagery," who must be brought to a state of civilization through education. The immediate plan by which to accomplish this was to establish Aboriginals in permanent settlements and commence instruction so that an agricultural form of lifestyle would be possible. Missionaries and schoolmasters were conscripted to instruct the children, to teach them to pray, to read the Scriptures, and to pursue "moral lives" (Friesen, 1991b: 14). In 1857, legislation to design education for Indians was passed entitled, An Act for the Gradual Civilization of the Indian, followed by another act in 1858, called the Civilization and Enfranchisement Act. On attaining nationhood, Canada passed her first Indian-related legislation, the Indian Act, in 1876. The government also attempted to address the issues of Native education and local government by passing the Indian Advancement Act in 1884, but neither its provisions nor program were clear (Frideres, 1988: 29; Frideres and Gadacz, 2001: 25).

East Coast Campaign

The campaign to transform Indian culture via schooling has a long history in Canada. It was highlighted by a series of divergent thrusts even though religious instruction and the promotion of literacy topped the list of objectives. It was difficult to attain any degree of literary success since First Nations were nomadic peoples who often did not remain long enough in one area so their children could be "properly educated." Eventually, a wide range of program alternatives to day schooling was undertaken, perhaps best described in colloquial terms as consisting of fits and starts in terms of initiation, operation, and failure. With each successive failure, a new program was devised and lasted only until it became clear to its organizers that their efforts and finances were literally being wasted. A brief description of developments in the various geographic regions of Canada will illustrate the shotgun approach to Native education that was undertaken.

From the beginning, early mission day schools were unsuccessful for lack of attendance; thus another approach was needed. One alternative plan was to send young Indian boys and girls directly to France for their education. It was conjectured that this way they would be "properly educated" and would return to their tribes and teach their people the French way of life. The results were not favorable; more often than not these young Aboriginals would return as misfits, unable to function in either society. By 1639 the practice was ended because scarcely a dozen had returned to the colony to assist the missionaries (Cornish, 1881; Hawthorn, 1967; Jaenen, 1986).

By the middle of the 17th century the Jesuits developed day schools known as "reductions" in permanent settlements in New France, and tried to lure Native students with a view to teaching them the Catholic faith and French culture. The schools were built close to mission stations and French settlements, and First Nations were expected to remain near these settlements so their children could be educated. The primary objective of these efforts was to satisfy the mandate of the French government who expected the Jesuits to assist in the building of durable colonies in eastern Canada.

The curriculum of the Jesuit schools consisted of religious studies, agriculture, and manual trades. The children did adapt to the French diet, manner of dress and other aspects of the French lifestyle, but they were never successful in agriculture or manual trades (Brookes, 1991). Simultaneously, an uncloistered women's order, the Ursulines, begun by Sister Marguerite Bourgeoys, instructed Indian girls in French manners and customs, household duties, reading and writing, and religion. Later they also added knitting and spinning. Indicative of the serious intent of the program and to their credit developers is the fact that they tried to provide instruction in these courses in Aboriginal languages. The Ursulines represented the vision of Marguerite Bourgeoys who arrived in New France in 1653 in response to a call from Governor Maisionneuve of Ville-Marie Montreal to start a school. Five years later Sister Bourgeoys opened a school for girls in a converted stable and eventually enrolled Aboriginal students as well. Although her primary targets were children of fur traders and explorers whose families lived in nearby settlements, she later expanded her mission to include the education of the "King's girls," namely young women who came from France to New France to seek mates. Bourgeoys attempted to provide them with the knowledge needed to live on the frontier by emphasizing Christian values, social graces, the three "R's," and "house-wifely skills" (Chalmers, 1974).

The schools designed and promoted by the religious orders were met with opposition from Aboriginal parents who objected to the omission of Native history and culture from the curriculum. The Indians were proud of their heritage and did not want to give it up easily. Parents also objected to sending very young children to school who they thought should remain at home for a few more years. The underlying plank of Jesuit education was francization with an emphasis on religion, agriculture, and trade apprenticeships. The methodology employed consisted of memory work, repetition, recitation, and the writing of examinations.

By 1763, New France was absorbed by the British Empire and the administration of Indian people was assigned to the British Imperial Government. This policy continued until 1830. The British military initially assumed this responsibility and functioned with the sole purpose of maintaining Indian allegiance and cooperation. The education of Indian people was left to the religious sector, and one such organization, The New England Company assumed control in New Brunswick. The leaders of the organization stressed three themes in their programs of instruction – English language teaching, religion, and vocational training. Administration of the program was located in England and governed by a board made up of learned men representing the judiciary, the clergy, merchants, and government leaders.

The New England Company encouraged Native parents to live near British settlements so that better management of their children could be facilitated. Since this arrangement forbad great indulgence in a nomadic way of life, parents were sometimes supplied with food, clothing and other provisions. A variety of educational approaches were undertaken by The New England Company, with an extensive use of Native languages such as Chippewa, Cree, and Micmac. One special feature included an apprenticeship program whereby Indian children would be sent to live with selected nonNative families in hopes that the youngsters would learn a trade. After fifteen years this program was shut down because on returning home not a single Indian youth had been successfully employed.

By the middle of the 19th century a number of church denominations were involved in Native education in eastern Canada with the double-edged objective of spreading the Gospel and "culturally rehabilitating the Indian." During the period from 1833 when missionary Peter Jones petitioned the Methodist Church to build a residential school among the Ojibway people of Ontario, to 1988 when last residential school in Canada closed (McKay Residential School in Dauphin, Manitoba), 80 such schools were in operation.

Western Campaign

With the fall of New France and the establishment of British sovereignty, a path was clear for the expansion of Protestant missions into other areas of the new country. By the mid-1800s most regions of Canada had been claimed by Anglican, Methodist, Presbyterian, and Roman Catholic missionaries. In British Columbia, Roman Catholic missions were established throughout the interior, while Anglican and Methodist missionaries competed for territory on the northern British Columbia coast. All three denominations joined Presbyterian efforts in western Canada.

The first recorded encounter of Europeans with the Aboriginal peoples of British Columbia is reported to have occurred in July 1774, when the Spanish navigator, Juan Pérez met a group of Haidas near Langara Island. Four years later, explorer Captain James Cook spent nearly a month refitting his ship at Nootka Sound, and engaged in trade with the local residents. By 1792, the west coast fur trade was in full swing with efforts concentrated on the more heavily settled south coast and Vancouver Island.

As was the custom, missionary educators arrived in the new territory shortly after the first explorers. Although educational efforts among First Nations of British Columbia began in the latter part of the 18th century, mission schools for Indians did not become populous in British Columbia until the middle of the 19th century. In 1838 a Roman Catholic missionary, Modeste Demers, undertook a reconnaissance survey of the interior of British Columbia and reported that the locals were quite receptive to educational endeavors (Furniss, 1995: 43). In 1849, The Reverend Robert Staines, a Church of England minister began a school at Fort Victoria for children of Hudson's Bay Company employees, while a Roman Catholic priest, Father Lempfrit, began a school for Métis children (Johnson, 1968: 62). In 1856, a self-styled non-ordained Anglican missionary, William Duncan, built a mission school among the Tsimshian at Fort Simpson (Duff, 1997: 136). In 1872 the Oblates made Fort Thompson the headquarters for their missionary efforts among local First Nations.

Shortly after establishing settlements in British Columbia, the missionaries moved inland towards the prairies. The Roman Catholic Church, represented by the Oblates, virtually dominated the early stages of the missionary education movement following their founding in the 1840s. They worked hand in hand with the Grey Nuns (Sisters of Charity) who were responsible for the education of Native girls. The first schools established by the Grey Nuns were at St. Boniface and Pembina, Manitoba, around 1817. The Pembina School lasted only six years while the one at St. Boniface lasted ten years. Within the decade itinerant missionaries, both Roman Catholic and Protestant, were involved in teaching Native and nonNative children in fur trading posts stretching from the United States to the Arctic (Lupul, 1970).

In the west a host of well-known missionaries labored for the same cause including James Evans, Robert Rundle, Father Albert Lacombe, Father Joseph Hugonnard, Henry Steinhauer (a Native missionary), and others. Typical of the educational philosophy of the time, Methodist missionaries George McDougall and his son, John, strove to "Christianize, educate and civilize" the Indians, in their case the Woodland Crees and the Stoneys (McDougall, 1903: 71). Father Hugonnard outlined his objective even more bluntly, namely to remove Indian boys and girls from their "savage milieu" and convert them to "civilized" habits through English language instruction (Gresko, 1979: 91)

The Hudson's Bay Company encouraged these efforts hoping that the civilizing effect of these institutions would auger well for their business interests. By 1857 the company was making annual grants to various religious denominations in an effort to encourage their educational endeavors. The Roman Catholics were the most aggressive, and after establishing their St. Boniface School, moved on to other locations. They began a school at Lac St. Anne in 1842, at Fort Edmonton in 1852, and at Lac La Biche in 1854. Father Albert Lacombe founded a permanent school in Fort Edmonton in 1860 with an enrollment of more than 20 children. Day schools generally turned out to be ineffective in terms of missionary objectives because these schools allowed only temporary contact with Aboriginal students. The missionaries argued that by removing students from their parents and incarcerating them in residential schools, "they could spend several years in acquiring regular habits of discipline and a taste and a liking for work" (Fisher, 1978: 138).

The first Protestant school in the North West Territory was initiated by Methodist James Evans on Playgreen Island at the Rossville Mission near Norway House. Two decades later George McDougall and his son, John, undertook missionary work among the Woodland Crees at Fort Victoria and the Stoney (Nakoda Sioux) Indians at Morley, Alberta (Friesen, 1974: 59).

After the Riel War of 1885, the temporary tenor of relations established between the Canadian government and First Nations withered somewhat as additional settlers poured into Native territory. As a result, Aboriginal people began to be a minority in the west, so federal officials felt free to impose a rigorous pattern of cultural assimilation. This policy of "coercive tutelage" was based on the assumption that Native people did not know and perhaps could not know what was in their best interests. It fell to government to strip them of their civil, economic, and cultural rights under a regime of government paternalism. Subcontracting the operation of Indian schools to religious denominations not only shed government of the responsibility of working in an area in which they had no expertise, but transferred some of the cost to the churches. Whenever the churches opted for the building of more residential schools the government somewhat disinterestedly demurred (Dyck, 1997: 14).

During David Goggin's reign as the first Superintendent of Education in the North West Territories from 1893 to 1912, he sought to develop a universal school system. As a strong British national imperialist he had little patience with the values of ethnic minorities or First Nations. His concern was that the children of these communities should grow up to be Canadians and learn to speak the language. As he put it, "A common school and a common tongue are essential if we are to have a homogeneous citizenship" (McDonald, 1974: 178).

The Persistence of Indian Education Policy

Since Confederation the creation of Indian education policy has consistently been a federal responsibility. As a prelude to his arrangement, in 1847 the Province of Canada published a report based on the ideas of Egerton Ryerson, Canada's first superintendent of English-speaking schools. Ryerson urged the government to adopt a policy whereby Aboriginals could be raised to the educational level of the EuroCanadians. This perspective motivated the new Canadian government of 1867 to maintain control of Indian affairs rather than relegate them to provincial administration.

Although the establishment of the Indian Act in 1876 authorized the federal government to provide schooling for First Nations, the responsibility was soon shifted to the church denominations who were already involved in the enterprise (Brookes, 1991: 168). The Canadian federal government had only been in operation for a decade so it seemed quite easy to delegate some areas of governance rather than fulfil them. Besides, it looked as though the long-range forecast for Indigenous survival was cultural genocide, so why bother providing them with a first-class education? Indian education policy, therefore, evolved without too much government planning.

In 1879 the Davin Report urged the establishment of residential schools following the pattern set in the United States. Thus, during the 1880s, the Canadian government shifted its Indian education policy from the creation of day schools to residential schools, and a number of such schools were established in British Columbia. By 1894, 11 residential schools were operating in British Columbia including one at Alert Bay (Wolcott, 1967), Kamloops (Haig-Brown, 1993), and Williams Lake (Furniss, 1995). A residential school was established at Mopass in Yukon Territory in 1901 (King, 1967).

A short-lived experiment in Native education was the development of industrial schools (Titley, 1992). These schools were begun shortly after 1830 when the civil branch of government took over Indian matters from the military. The industrial schools differed from residential schools by attempting preparation in trades as a means of preparing Indian youth for a new way of life. The fur trade was over and in order to assist Indian people to ward off destruction and ruin, their children would need to learn skills required in the new world. The boys were taught such trades as shoemaking, carpentry, blacksmithing, and tailoring. The girls learned sewing, knitting, washing, and cooking.

Essentially, the industrial schools failed. After a few years of operation it became evident that few of the students were applying the skills they learned in their daily lives. Some of the factors that led to this dismal conclusion included late enrolment for many students, parental prejudice against the schools, short periods of attendance, and lack of funds to establish "graduates" when they completed their term of studies. Native parents basically resented residential industrial schools. They did not like their children being taken away from them, often very far away. They also disliked the deliberate attempts to "convert and civilize" their children whom they wanted to retain in the lineage of their cultural heritage. They also resented the restrictions on the use of Indian languages and the teaching of "women's chores" to young men (Gresko, 1979). Fortunately for them, only a small portion of First Nations young people attended residential schools although those who attended day schools were philosophically and culturally not much better off. Aboriginal children were provided with negative perspectives about their heritage in both settings. Parents who did favor either residential or day schools often did so because they thought their children were mainly being taught how to read and write (Miller, 1987: 3f). They objected to the work component of the industrial schools believing that their offspring were being short-changed. After all, they were being sent to school to learn literary skills, not to become unpaid apprentices with full-time jobs.

Twentieth Century Developments

By 1920 amendments to the 1876 Indian Act mandated compulsory schooling for Native children at either day or residential schools, and it was not until 1946 that concern about cultural genocide was raised. J. Allison Glen, Minister of Mines and Resources suggested that as much as possible, First Nations children should be given the opportunity to retain as many Native characteristics as possible while developing the ability to function as full-fledged Canadian citizens.

In 1947, New Zealand anthropologist, Diamond Jenness urged the Canadian government to "solve the Indian problem" by abolishing Indian reserves and establishing an integrated approach to schooling. The underlying intent of Jenness' plan was to assimilate the Indians and thereby "eliminate the Indian problem within twenty-five years" (Haig-Brown, 1993: 32). Subsequent modifications to the Indian Act in 1951 changed little, except to make it possible for Aboriginal children to attend public schools. Before another line of attack was devised, plans were made to turn over the administration of residential schools directly into the hands of government bureaucrats instead of religious leaders. By the 1960s this arrangement had pretty well been concluded.

The process of transforming administration of residential schools to secular control began in 1949. That year a Special Joint Committee of the Senate and the House of Commons recommended that wherever possible Indian children should be educated in association with nonNative children (Friesen, 1983: 48). The committee solicited the advice of Native leaders and obtained 411 briefs in all. The proposals were distributed among Native communities for added input. Finally, government leaders thought they had achieved two-way communication. Now the path was cleared for integrated education. The bottom line was that education following the traditional European format was still perceived as the vehicle by which the assimilation of First Nations could come about (Hawthorn, 1967). Most Aboriginal parents would be invited to sit on advisory boards, but they would not have an official voice in either educational policy-making or school procedure. Integration in this mode was to be the order of the day.

On March 15, 1967 the Honorable Arthur Laing, Minister of Indian Affairs and Northern Development, announced a seven-point integration program for Indian education. The plan was to work collaboratively with provincial departments of education to integrate Native children into provincial schools. Laing promised more consultation with First Nations parents than had been the case before, by inviting them to sit on school boards in districts where a significant number of Aboriginal children were enrolled (Burns, 1998). Standardized forms of provincial curricula were to be used and amended only when special needs of students became apparent. Federal schools were to follow suit. Residential schools were to be continued in use only when absolutely necessary, and then with full consultation with the religious organizations that ran them (Ashworth, 1979: 39-40).

Laing's proposals were studied for four years and reported on in 1971 with the conclusion that the sooner Indigenous pupils left federal schools and entered provincial schools, the better their chances of enjoying academic advances. The key factor would be for Native students to become fluent in the official langauge of the school. It was also noted that unless the school offered instruction in Native languages through the high school level, those students would lose knowledge of their Native language altogether.

Barman (1986) contends that nonNative Canadians have never wanted First Nations to enter their socio-economic order, and this has motivated them to offer an inferior kind of education in Native communities. In most

Canadians' minds, Indians are to remain at the bottom rung of the economic ladder and not compete on even ground with their fellow nonNatives. This suggests that if Indian youth triumph by surviving the residential school, they will only encounter additional road-blocks and discrimination further ahead. The bottom line is that Indian children were orginally imprisoned on the pretext of educating them, while in reality their potential to develop fully as members of either Native or nonNative society was squelched.

White Paper, Red Paper

When the Liberal government took office in 1968 under the leadership of Pierre Elliott Trudeau, Ottawa bureaucrats decided to adopt a brand new, modern-oriented Indian policy. The intent was to resolve once and for all the issue of Indian land claims so that the legal base for such claims would vanish forever. No longer would Aboriginals be treated differently than other Canadians. The economic status of Indian people would be ungraded to complete individual self-reliance along with other Canadians. Essentially, this meant the elimination of Indian Status in order to transform Indians into Canadians in the same sense as other Canadians (Boldt, 1993: 18).

The historical background to the White Paper, Red Paper controversy dates to 1963 when the federal government asked University of British Columbia anthropologist, Harry Hawthorn, to survey the living conditions of Canada's Native peoples. The observations made by Hawthorn's (1966-1967) team of researchers stunned everyone, including government leaders. The report pointed out the devastating conditions under which most Canadian Indians were living. The report showed that Indians suffered from unemployment, poverty, health problems, and even malnutrition. Their housing was substandard, education was inadequate, and their life expectancy was dismally below that of other Canadians. Hawthorn made a plea that Aboriginal people be extended the same rights as other citizens and be assured that their legal status be honored as well. This observation later gave rise to the phrase, "Citizen's Plus," implying that First Nations were Canadian citizens who had special additional rights.

During the 1960s in Canada there was a great deal of discussion about human rights and fundamental freedoms of citizens in general. The American civil rights movement spilled over into Canada and forced attention on neglected minorities. The Red Power movement and Vietnam War demonstrations in the United States threatened many Canadians who feared that similar protests might develop in this Canada. The armed occupation of Anicinabe Park in Kenora, Ontario, and the near riot on Parliament Hill were proof that the same thing could happen here (Purich, 1986: 188). The theme of the 1960s movement targeted needy minorities and stressed the provision of opportunities for neglected communities in an effort to bring them up to with the rest of society. Unfortunately, this implied that all responsibility to make emendations to motivation or lifestyle to fit the mainstream lay within the minority camp. Central to this position was the assumption that education would be the vehicle by which to accomplish this goal. Good teaching and good education would serve to equalize opportunity and minimize differences (Friesen, 1993b: 7).

Against this background, in 1969 the Canadian federal government decided it was time for a radical shift in Indian policy. It was a move that represented blatant assimilation. To implement this view, the Honorable Jean Chrétien, Minister of Indian Affairs and Northern Development, issued a White Paper outlining the government's new view on Indian affairs. The underlying assumption was that the Aboriginal Peoples of Canada were to join the rest of Canadians by having their special status eliminated via proposed legislation. The major recommendations of the report included abolition of the Department of Indian Affairs and Northern Development (DIAND), repeal of the Indian Act, and the transfer of Indian programs to provincial administration. Management of Indian reserve lands was to be turned over directly to Indian bands. The government also proposed to formulate a policy to end treaties. The insulting tone of the report became evident when Ottawa patronizingly agreed to recognize the contributions that the Indigenous People had made to Canadian society (White Paper, 1969).

The government White Paper was vigorously opposed by First Nations who were joined in their repudiation by a number of nonNative social and political organizations (Cardinal, 1969). The first official reaction to the White Paper came in the form of the Red Paper in 1970, authorized by the Indian chiefs of Alberta. The Red Paper criticized every one of the points made in the White Paper claiming that it was a document of despair, not hope. The framers of the Red Paper contended that if the proposals of the White Paper went through, within a generation or two Indians would be left with no land and the threat of complete assimilation. Strong criticism of the Red Paper was launched in a book, *Ruffled Feathers,* by Cree lawyer, William Wuttunee (1971) of Calgary, who accused the writers of fostering a treaty mentality and supporting a buckskin and feather culture. It soon became public that the Red Paper was actually prepared by M & M Systems Research of Alberta, an organization established by former Social Credit Premier, Ernest Manning, and his son (Wuttunee, 1971: 58).

A second major paper which was critical of the White Paper emanated from the Union of British Columbia Indian Chiefs, and became known as the Brown Paper. This group was concerned that the special relationship which had developed between First Nations and the federal government through the years should not be negated. The framers of the Brown Paper insisted that this relationship carried immense moral and legal force and should constitute the foundation for future cooperative policy-making. Interestingly, the Brown Paper also made reference to the principle of self-determination and suggested that Indian bands take over aspects of reserve administration at local levels. In this they joined with other Native organizations who requested the Indian Affairs Branch to provide necessary financial resources to develop their plans, programs, and budgets towards that end.

National Indian Brotherhood Response

Yet another form of protest to the White Paper came from the National Indian Brotherhood (NIB), now known as the Assembly of First Nations (AFN). The NIB originated during the 1960s when the federal government decided to fund Native organizations to provide an avenue through which Native people could express their views. The NIB was preceded by the National Indian Council (NIC) which represented the concerns of both Status Indians and Métis. With the origin of the NIB to represent Status Indians, the Canadian Métis Society was then formed to represent Métis and nonStatus interests. These and other, newer organizations experienced some success through lobbying, organizing, and protesting. In response to these pressures, in 1970 the federal government decided not to proceed with implementing the White Paper (Purich, 1986: 187). Thus the veiled campaign to assimilate First Nations was compelled to continue in another vein.

The NIB response to the White Paper had a silver lining in terms of a proposed educational policy. The background to this proposal included some very unique events in northeastern Alberta. Native parents at St. Paul, Alberta, some of them educated in residential schools themselves, had grown increasingly involved in the education of their children. Not content merely to act in an advisory capacity, and then only regarding such matters as school lunch programs or bussing, these parents continued their campaign for greater involvement. Things came to a head in 1970 when nearly 300 Native people conducted a sit-in at the Blue Quills School in St. Paul Alberta. Reluctantly, the government gave in to the demands of the promoters of the three-month long event, and the first locally-controlled school in Canada came to be (Persson, 1986; Bashford and Heinzerling, 1987). By 1975 ten Indian band councils were operating their own schools and by 1985 two-thirds of reserve schools across the nation were either partly or completely managed by Aboriginal school boards.

In 1972 the NIB followed up on the Blue Quills event by issuing an education policy dealing with four broad issues. The *first* concern identified by the NIB was to wrest control of Indian schools away from external agencies and manage them locally. *Second,* the NIB raised the matter of curriculum relevancy, arguing that local education should make reference to local historical events and happenings. In other words, they wanted the curriculum to reflect elements of Aboriginal history and culture. They requested that all future curricular innovations, teaching methods, and the nature of pupil-teacher relationships should have parental approval.

A *third* concern of the NIB was the matter of teacher training in institutions of higher learning. Their report argued that it was difficult to procure knowledgable or culturally-sensitive teachers because relevant training was not available in Canadian university and colleges. *Fourth,* and finally, the NIB pointed out that educational facilities in most Native communities were pitiful when compared to those in nonNative communities, and the government should seek to address these concerns (Kirkness, 1981).

Several encouraging changes came about as a result of the NIB's policy paper, and the future began to look more promising for the First Nations of Canada. School dropout rates and absenteeism generally decreased and a greater number of Aboriginal children were enrolled in public school systems. Parental involvement in school affairs increased and additional Indian band councils took charge of their local schools. The federal government appeared sympathetic to these developments and dozens of new schools were built in Native communities. The matter of teacher preparation was still a concern because teacher training institutions were slow to develop needed programs.

Assembly of First Nations Response

In 1988 the Assembly of First Nations (AFN) conducted a comprehensive community-based review of the status of Aboriginal education in Canada. The result was a four volume report, *Tradition and Education: Towards a Vision of Our Future,* containing 54 recommendations. The report called on Canadians to recognize the inherent right of First Nations to maintain their unique cultural identity and to exercise control over their local educational systems. The AFN unanimously passed a resolution to back the intent of the report which outlined the need for local jurisdiction over education in Indigenous communities.

The foundational plank of the AFN report had to do with Aboriginal self-government. First Nations were currently demanding a return to the days when they governed all of their affairs, including education. Their argument was that governance over only one segment of community life (education) begged the question of Aboriginal self-government. Until the federal government and Native leaders agreed what constitutes Aboriginal self-government, however, First Nations would continue to be frustrated in their attempt to exercise control over their operations. Allocation of resources was a major concern because if purse strings were continued to be held by the Department of Indian Affairs, band control did not really exist.

Change does occur, however, and at the present time, Native communities *do* have jurisdiction over educational policy, management methods and approaches, curriculum standards, program quality, and delivery service. Indian bands can even determine total education resource requirements, including capital and operational requirements, but only in the field of education (Tremblay, 2001: 17). This is still a far way from realizing complete Aboriginal self-government, but it does show that some progress has been made in the last decade. In 1993 First Nations had only three options open to them. *First,* they could maintain the status quo; *second,* they could try to have access to funding by which to run their own schools (which they have attained), or *third,* they could attempt to establish closer links with provincial systems (Goddard, 1992: 165)

The DIAND responded to the AFN report by appointing James Macpherson to review *Traditional and Education: Towards a Vision of Our Future* and make recommendations. Macpherson immediately discovered that the exercise of authority over education by First Nations had no independent constitutional foundation and recommended that one be included in the Constitution of Canada. He pointed out Indian jurisdiction over Indian education should comprise the pivotal point of negotiations about reform in Aboriginal education. This observation was premised on the reality that the Canadian government should accept and move ahead on First Nations self-government in Canada. Macpherson proposed that a constitutional amendment be made with regard to the fundamental relationship between Canada and First Nations. Following that, a national education statute should be installed that would improve the structure of education delivery systems and the quality of education for Native students in Canada (Tremblay, 2001: 30). Macpherson outlined four possible models by which reform in the field of Native education could be realized and he outlined specific steps for the government to take in this regard.

The Macpherson Report recommended that First Nations devise and submit their own definition of Aboriginal self-government so that after negotiation, the definition could be included in the Canadian Constitution. Consequently the Aboriginal people would be able to establish educational policies that would be more compatible with their philosophy and beliefs.

The report also recommended that the government increase funding for Indian education and establish in-service programs for nonNative teachers wishing to work in Native communities.

The Royal Commission on Aboriginal Peoples

In 1991 the federal government established the Royal Commission on Aboriginal Peoples (RCAP), something which Prime Minister Brian Mulroney had offered Elijah Harper and his supporters in June 1990, when the Meech Lake Accord was struck down in the Manitoba Legislature. Chaired by former AFN Chief George Erasmus and Quebec Judge René Dussault, the Commission included both Native and nonNative member commissioners. A number of public meetings were held, transcripts were analyzed and a great deal of research was undertaken. Both the structure of the report and public hearings showed that the commissioners regarded their task as an exercise in public education as well as a government investigation (Miller, 2000: 385).

The RCAP completed its report in 1996. It consisted of five volumes, over 3 500 pages and 400 recommendations. The report took over five years to prepare at a cost of over 50 million dollars. In response to the Report's recommendations, in 1998, the Liberal government, under the leadership of Prime Minister Jean Chrétien, set up a special healing fund in the amount of 350 million dollars as a token of the government's apology for the treatment of Aboriginals in residential schools. The fund was to be used over a four year period. In addition, the government approved an increase of 250 million dollars in the next year's budget as a means of supporting the Aboriginal cause.

The essence of the RCAP Report was to recommend a major reconstruction of Canadian society so that justice and equality would be better assured for Aboriginal Canadians. Two urgent concerns of the report had to do with the number of suicides in Native communities and the assurance of fair criminal justice. The Commission recommended swift action in these areas, starting with meetings of the various bars, law societies, and law associations. It urged increased government expenditures in preventative programs.

Constitutionally speaking, the RCAP recommended re-writing the principles of the Royal Proclamation to reflect the new nation-to-nation concept of negotiation as well as a new foundation by which to perceive the past treaty-making process. The Commission also proposed the formation of an Aboriginal parliament as a first step towards creating a House of First peoples as the third chamber of the Parliament of Canada. This parliament would be primarily advisory and would have no lawmaking authority. The Commission also recommended the abolition of the Department of Indian Affairs and Northern Development to be replaced by two departments, that is, the Department of Aboriginal Relations and the Department of Indian and Inuit Services.

A number of other structures were also recommended by the RCAP. These included an Aboriginal Peoples' International University along with Aboriginal student unions and Aboriginal residential colleges. An Aboriginal Languages Foundation would parallel the work of the international university and supplement its efforts to maintain Aboriginal languages and culture.

Clearly the RCAP Report represents the most comprehensive effort to date undertaken by government on behalf of the Indigenous community. Only time will tell which of the many recommendations will see fruition. As Ponting (1997: 470) notes, "The rebalancing of political and economic power between Aboriginal nations and the Canadian governments represents the core of the hundreds of recommendations contained in this report."

Most Métis, Inuit, and nonStatus Indians were critical of the RCAP Report because most government action recommended in the report favored Status indians. Phil Fontaine, Grand Chief of the AFN at that time, generally approved of the government's actions suggesting that they were the best one could hope for at the time.

Thomas Flanagan (2000), Professor of Political Science at the University of Calgary has been an outspoken critic of the RCAP Report taking issue with its foundational assumptions. Flanagan refuses to accept the premise that Aboriginals differ from other Canadians because they were here first. He argues that before the European invasion of North America, Aboriginal peoples were almost in constant motion and in perpetual competition with one another for land. He also contests the notion that before European contact, First Nations possessed sovereignty. He bases his argument on a definition of statehood that includes sovereignty only as a corollary attribute. Flanagan argues that Aboriginal Peoples cannot be considered nations in the sense that they are subordinate communities within the nation of Canada. In addition, statements about self-government usually assume community. Any argument about permanent Indian communities that predate the arrival of Europeans has to assume that the various Aboriginal communities have been living in the same locations under the same governments for thousands of years. In fact, they moved around a lot and their arrival on this continent probably stems from at least three migrations at three different times (Flanagan, 2000: 23).

Flanagan also attacks a fundamental premise of current land claim proponents who argue that Aboriginal property rights should be recognized as full ownership rights in Canadian law. He points out that the language of contemporary land claims needs to be modernized and reinterpreted to recognize the reality of an ongoing relationship between two parties. His solution for Aboriginal economic prosperity is for full integration of Indian peoples into the modern economy. This implies a willingness to leave the reserves, if necessary, and relocate to where jobs and investment opportunities exist (Flanagan, 2000: 7).

Education Proposals

The Royal Commission on Aboriginal Affairs reviewed many aspects of Native education including holistic learning, teacher education, elder involvement, education for self-government, and new partnerships in First Nations education. Leaning heavily on the premise of education for self-government, the report proposed a two-phased model of a First Nations education system. In the first phase the government would acknowledge that education would be a primary channel through which to achieve self-government jurisdiction. In this phase local Native communities would be motivated to undertake initiatives to achieve self-government.

The second phase of the RCAP report recommended a reconstitution of Indian bands to put them in a better position to assume administration of local education. In some instances, for example, this might require the merger of smaller Indian bands. While reconstitution was going on the government would provide extra funds for the process and conduct an ongoing dialogue with Native communities to ensure ideational compatibility.

Standing Senate Committee on Aboriginal Peoples Response

A further response by the federal government to the proposals of the RCAP came in the form of a study undertaken by the Standing Senate Committee on Aboriginal Peoples (SSCAP). The purpose of the study was to provide opportunity for public reaction and formulate specific recommendations. The committee was particularly concerned that unresolved jurisdictional issues could seriously hamper a full realization of Aboriginal educational self-government. To this end the committee recommended the establishment of an Office of Aboriginal Relations with two main divisions – a Treaty and Agreements Negotiation Division, and a Treaty and Agreements Implementation Secretariat. The office would operate outside of the DIAND, with the hope that the DIAND could eventually be dissolved. The DIAND would then be replaced with a more streamlined government agency responsible for discharging the legal, fiduciary, and constitutional obligations of the

Crown arising from the treaties and other agreements with Aboriginal peoples. The Standing Senate Committee on Aboriginal Peoples appropriately, recommended that judges, senior officials, and lawyers working with various levels of the judiciary in Canada be given opportunities for cross-cultural training to enable them to enhance their awareness of the various facets of the Aboriginal milieu. The training would include emphasis on Native history and culture, Aboriginal rights and treaty law, as well as First Nations' perspectives on related matters (Tremblay, 2001: 42-43).

Encouraging agreements that reflect the intent of the federal government to implement Aboriginal education self-government include the Framework Agreement on Indian Education in Manitoba (1990), the Umbrella Final Agreement with the Council for Yukon Indians (1993), the Nisga's Final Agreement (1993), and the Mi'kmaq Education Act (1998). There are several challenges to be worked out in initiating the above reforms. *First* and foremost is the fact that the definition of Aboriginal self-government per se has never been agreed by both government and Native leaders. Progress has been made with regard to Indian educational jurisdiction and there is now unanimity. A *second* concern is the reality that the federal government alone has jurisdiction over funding. Severe curtailing of needed funds to any component of the proposed program could delay or derail important developments. *Third*, is the matter of achieving unanimity in the Indian constituency particularly in regard to such complex issues as defining Aboriginal self-government. A united Indian front could work towards convincing the federal government to negotiate conscientiously with Native organizations. Although it has always been the intent of the Assembly of First Nations to represent the various Indigenous communities across Canada, many bands still refuse to acknowledge this representation.

Any discussion of Aboriginal self-government must include reference to Indian lands and Indian land claims. While Indigenous lands are currently being held in trust by the federal government, and no individual band can initiate any action with regard to management sale thereof, it is sometimes frustrating for Indian bands to influence government decisions pertaining to use of lands. The key issue with regard to Native land claims is a subjective one, namely the political intent government. This is strongly influenced by the will of the Canadian people and the reaction by government to what they perceive is public opinion. There is no doubt that a better informed public would incline a more sincere attitude on the part of government to do right by the Indigenous peoples of Canada. This challenge needs to be taken up by Aboriginal people themselves. No party is better qualified to define their needs and represent their interests, and no one stands to gain more by the process.

Six

The Residential School Phenomenon

Indian residential schools were the product of the nineteenth-century federal policy of assimilation. (Furniss, 1995: 15)

Our object is to continue until there is not a single Indian in Canada that has not been absorbed into the body politic and there is no Indian question, and no Indian department, that is the whole object of the bill–statement in 1920 by Deputy Superintendent General Duncan Campbell Scott. (Haig-Brown, 1993: 31-32)

There were years of slavery as residential schools were supported by child labor; humiliation was the experience of every Indian child who attended one of these schools. (Grant, 1996: 17)

Those who ran the school tried to rob us of our collective identity by punishing us for speaking our language, calling us "savages" and "heathens." (Knockwood, 1994: 157)

The residential school was . . . designed to separate Indian children from their families so they could be systematically fitted with the religious beliefs, social habits, and educational training that would turn them into "little brown white men." (Dyck, 1997: 14)

Badly built and ill-maintained, they were both the cause and the context of a dreadful crisis in sanitation and health. (Milloy, 1999: 75)

A special place must be reserved in perdition for those who abused residential school students sexually. (Miller, 2000: 423)

Many Native people remember with deep pain the experiences they suffered during their time at the ill-famed residential schools. As may be inferred from the above quotations, literature pertaining to the phenomenon of residential schools is growing rapidly documenting what historian John S. Milloy (1999) has called "a national crime." Personal stories related by former inmates of the system emphasize the inhumane conditions of these assimilation-oriented institutions, including child labor, personal humiliation, language loss, poor sanitation and health conditions, and sexual abuse.

The sad irony is that these tortured individuals were supposed to be inculcating the virtues of Christianity and European civilization. The reality was that this form of education dictated long absences from home. Some children never saw their parents for periods of time ranging from four to seven years, and in some cases even longer, depending on individual "success." Life in the residential school meant participating in an entirely different cultural milieu, replete with such alien features as corporal punishment, strict discipline, hard work, loneliness, and, worst of all, confinement. On the positive side (if there is one), residential schools *did* provide some training in EuroCanadian-centred language arts and today many Aboriginal leaders can trace their literary beginnings to the years they spent in residential schools. Assembly of First Nations' leaders, Phil Fontaine and Matthew Coon Come, for example, are both former students of residential schools. In interviews with former students in residential schools, Bull (1991: 40) identified at least a few positive memories.

> Some Native students who enjoyed the vocational or industrial aspect of the curriculum were those employed in the "domestic" section. For example, one male in the bakery preferred this "practical aspect" and some females liked sewing. . . . On reflection, another "good" experience was that these Native students made friends with other children from other tribes and reserves. It was difficult to communicate initially in cases where Native languages were different, but once they had made the emotional bond between them, the students kept in connection all their lives.

The fact that some students had positive memories of some activities does not in any way justify the operations of residential schools, but it might offer at least a little consolation to those who in spite of the system benefitted from it. Cooper (1999: book jacket) stretches the parameters of belief when he suggests that "For some, like renowned Olympian and football star Jim Thorpe and physician Susan La Flesche, an Indian school education [in a residential school] led to success and prosperity." For the vast majority, however, life in residential schools offered isolating, alienating, and frightening experiences.

Today former residential school inmates still meet to reminisce and comfort one another. In some ways the bond they made with their fellow sufferers has served partially to alleviate the pain of the memory of the cruelties and hardships endured during their years of incarceration.

Origins of the System

The background to the formation of residential schools in Canada developed over many decades. The first schools for Indian children were operated by the Hudson's Bay Company which built them primarily for the children of their employees. Few Native children were actually enrolled. A second group operating schools for Aboriginal students were missionaries. By the 1630s the Jesuits had built a school for Huron children at Quebec City, established a mission, and encouraged the development of a series of agricultural villages. As earlier stated, Sister Marguerite Bourgeoys, who later founded the Order of Ursulines, arrived in New France in 1653 in response to a call from Governor Maisionneuve of Ville-Marie Montreal. Five years after her arrival Sister Bourgeoys opened a school for girls in a converted stable and eventually enrolled Native children as well. Although her primary targets were children of fur traders and explorers whose families lived in nearby settlements. (Chalmers, 1974).

In 1763 when New France fell and the English took over, Protestant denominations also became involved in Native education. The conclusion of the War of 1812, contributed to significant economic changes in the country and the fur trade was greatly affected. Now, instead of being viewed as allies, First Nations were seen as obstacles to the nation's progress. Increases in European immigration led to conflicts over land, and loss of hunting, trapping, and fishing grounds contributed to poverty among First Nations. Social humanitarian ideologies that arose during the 1800s drew attention to the Indians' plight stressing the need for basic literacy, and agricultural and industrial skills (Furniss, 1995: 19-21).

The spiritual and psychological conquest of the First Peoples of Canada via schooling produced many devastating results. Although the campaign to squelch the culture of First Nations was more militarily-deliberate in the United States, in many ways the Canadian crusade took on all the earmarks of a conquest of bloodshed. When the fur trade began to diminish the role of Indigenous peoples changed. No one had postulated what a post fur trade culture might be like nor laid plans for life following its aftermath. French imperialists were a bit of an exception in that they demonstrated an attitude which at least partially set the stage for the development of a new nation (the Métis) through planned racial amalgamation (Sealey and Lussier, 1975: 17).

The implications of the dwindling fur trade were far-reaching in consequence (Ray, 1974). The shift in economy affected all sectors of society and hunting and gathering no longer had a place in the new world. Agriculture and industrial development replaced traditional forms of livelihood and urban dwellers became a phenomenon. Because the Aboriginal people found it difficult to gain any degree of satisfaction in any of these sectors, a place had to be found for them. Without too much analysis, the invaders concluded that the cultures of the First Nations should be transformed into European forms of civilization. The formula for initiating them into the new society featured residential schooling made up of an admixture of government funding and religious administration.

Pre-Confederation Practices

By the middle of the 19th century a number of church denominations in Canada were involved in Native education with the double-edged objective of spreading the Gospel and "culturally rehabilitating the Indian." The Catholic Church, represented by the Oblates, virtually dominated the early stages of the missionary education movement following their founding in the 1840s. A few years later Anglican and Methodist missionaries also entered the area.

The Oblates worked with the Grey Nuns and together they established mission posts across northern Alberta and preserved a French Catholic presence in the west. The Grey Nuns moved to St. Albert in 1863, following Father Albert Lacombe, and built an orphanage, convent, and school there. Later on they added a hospital. The Grey Nuns were among the first educated nonNative women in Alberta and their legacy includes the founding of the General Hospital in Edmonton and the Holy Cross Hospital in Calgary.

Not everyone involved in the enterprise of making the Indian over shared the reductionist view that an assimilative recipe combining the message of the Christian religion with schooling would accomplish their complete acculturation. Some government bureaucrats saw the Indigenous People as unfortunate victims of the times and felt sorry for them. Incoming settlers perceived them as intruders, occupiers of lands more suitable for farming than nomadic hunting. Do-gooders pitied them as "strangers within their own country." In the final analysis, Indians were the "white man's burden" desperately in need of gaining a toehold on 20th century civilization; fortunately, their "salvation" was possible through His Majesty's Christian influence (Surtees, 1969).

When the success rate of the campaign to make farmers of Native youth via day schooling indicated "low returns," Roman Catholic priests turned their attention to the establishment of "seminaries" or boarding (residential) schools. Indian parents were naturally reluctant to part with their children for lengthy periods of time and the missionaries often had to bribe them into letting their children go. A special aspect of this program was to enroll some

French children in Native schools as a means of encouraging Indian pupils to take on French cultural ways. Indian parents objected to this deliberate socialization plan wanting instead to teach their children their ancestral beliefs and culture. Still, the push to have residential schools for Indian children continued, and by the end of the 19th century every region of the nation had boarding schools for Indian children, financed by the government, with the church providing spiritual guidance and management. This move was promoted by Egerton Ryerson who in 1844 became the first superintendent of schools in English-speaking Canada. Ryerson promoted the idea that the First Nations could not accomplish civilization without a "religious feeling" and thus "the animating and controlling spirit of each residential school should be a religious one" (Brookes, 1991: 20). The Province of Canada endorsed Ryerson's plan, acknowledging "the superiority of the European culture and the need to raise them [Aboriginals] to the level of the whites" (Haig-Brown, 1993: 29).

One of the highlights of missionary work in the mid 19th century was the founding of a successful Aboriginal agricultural settlement at Credit River in southern Ontario by Methodist missionary Peter Jones. Jones (Sacred Feathers, or Kahkewaquonaby in Ojibway), was a young man of part Ojibway heritage who lived with his nonNative father until he was 21 years of age. At that point he became the Methodist Church's spokesman and helped attract Ojibway converts to serve as preachers, interpreters, and schoolteachers. It was through his efforts that the Methodist Church extended their mission westward from Ontario (Rogers, 1994: 125-126).

Jones convinced Indian leaders that building schools (day schools as well as residential schools), for Aboriginal children would assist the First Nations in adjusting to rapidly changing economic conditions. Band leaders readily bought into Jones' plan which was financed by government monies made available through the office of the Rev. Egerton Ryerson, Chief Superintendent of Common Schools for Upper Canada. At first Native leaders cooperated with the development of residential schools, however, they soon discovered that the educational objectives of those who ran these institutions were radically different from those desired by Indian leaders. Aboriginal parents thought the schools would teach their young skills necessary to enter the labor force of the industrial age. Instead the children were being primarily taught the Christian faith while being robbed of their language and cultural heritage. Indian resistance to missionary education peaked in 1863 so government officials pushed for legislation to enforce compulsory attendance. During this time a public system of education was being developed for nonNative Upper Canada, but Aboriginal children were educated in separate schools. When nonAboriginal settlers obtained government funds to build schools for their own children, Native children were not allowed to attend them. Sadly, the denominationally-run schools in the east later became the model for those developed in western Canada as well.

Post-Confederation Policy

Canadian Indian policy was actually rooted in British practices at the time when Great Britain was in control of this country. Prior to 1830 the British War Department handled Indian affairs, virtually ignoring their economic and social needs. Consequently, conditions in Native communities were deplorable. No longer needed for the fur trade, the First Nations found themselves fraught with disease and hunger, rapidly becoming a landless people. Their numbers were decreasing at an alarming rate and the British Colonial Office felt the "Indian problem" would soon be solved by the Indigenous people dying out. British ethnocentrism was the order of the day, and those who thought that something ought to be done for the Native people believed assimilation to be the best route. Thus in 1860 the Indian Department became part of the Crown Lands Department and shortly thereafter the position of Deputy Superintendent of Indian Affairs was created. Legislation entitled, the Act for the Gradual Civilization of Indian Tribes in Canada was passed and responsibility for Indian affairs was transferred from military to civil authority (Grant, 1996: 57).

In 1867, when Canada officially became a country in her own right, the responsibility for educating Native youth (as well as all others), fell to the new government. True, the treaties signed shortly thereafter, specified the provision of schooling for Indian children, but the approach and mode was not specifically spelled out, that is, "Her Majesty agrees to maintain schools for instruction in such reserves" (Brookes, 1991: 168). An underlying governmental assumption was that the long-range forecast for Aboriginal survival was eventually cultural genocide, so why bother providing a first-class education? Since missionaries were already involved in the enterprise, why not merely finance the continuance of their schools until they were no longer required? Naturally, religious denominations were overjoyed with the arrangement and even competed with one another for students.

In 1868, in tune with legislation, the government authorized allocations of money "to schools frequented by Indians." At this point the government funded 57 schools, only two of which were residential (Milloy, 1999: 52). Then the number of residential schools skyrocketed. In 1894 the government was funding 45 residential schools, 11 of them in British Columbia. By 1923 there were 71 such schools, and at their peak in the 1930s there were as many as 80 of them in operation. Sixty-five of these schools were located west of Ontario. The Roman Catholic Church ran 44 schools, the Anglicans ran 21, the United Church of Canada ran 10, and the Presbyterians ran two. Other, less well-known denominations ran the remaining three schools.

Although educators and religious leaders perceived of permanent Indian settlements (reserves) as more conducive to effective assimilation-oriented education, reality dictated that the establishment of reserves would free up lands for settlement by incoming Europeans. The reserve arrangement was administratively convenient for governmental provision of services to Indians even though few industries were developed to sustain the Indian economy on reserves (Melling, 1967). Without a functional outlet for the skills attained through education a sense of hopelessness pervaded the Indian community, coupled with the realization that a "thorough" education implied a total lack of acknowledgement of traditional Indian culture. Despite these developments, the Indian people did not take quickly to attempted changes, neither did they acquiesce to dying out (Patterson, 1972).

One of the first tasks the new Canadian government set for itself was to arrange for the First Nations to sign treaties regarding Indian lands. With this out of the way the new nation hoped to determine her boundaries and get on with the business of governing the new territory. Ten major treaties were therefore signed with First Nations in western Canada. Treaty No. 1 was signed in Manitoba with the Peguis (Ojibway) First Nation in 1871, six more treaties were completed during the 1870s, and three more followed in the 1880s. In 1876 the federal government passed the Indian Act which formalized federal dealings with First Nations. The act also defined who was an Indian and gave government officials the authority to impose a form of elected local band governance on Indian reserves.

Treaty signing was basically a peaceful process even though many Indian leaders were not pleased with the terms presented. Some bargained for a better deal while others gave in for the sake of peace. The content of the treaties basically pertained to lands given up, the assignment of reserves, and the provision of tools, seed, farm animals and ammunition. It was agreed that the government would provide some form of schooling for Native youth, but its exact nature was not specified. As it turned out the schools were financed by government but operated by various religious organizations. The Canadian federal government authorized commissioner Nicholas Flood Davin, to initiate a report regarding industrial schools in the United States. These special schools had been established to teach Native American youth relevant trades. When Davin reported to the Canadian government he urged the development of a system of residential schools in Canada as a method of assimilating the First Nations. Davin recommended that Indian children be incarcerated in residential schools as soon as they were of school age. As he stated, " . . . if anything is to be done with the Indian, we must catch him very young" (Haig-Brown, 1993: 30)

Davin's objective for a system of Indian residential schools was twofold. *First*, he believed these schools would assist in depriving Aboriginal children of their simple Indian mythology by a "process of civilization." The underlying pedagogical principle on which he built this objective was that one should not take away without substituting something positive. Davin sincerely believed that the Aboriginal people would be appreciative of what they were being taught as a substitute for traditional ways. The *second* aspect of Davin's objective was that residential schools should be turned over to religious denominations in order to fulfil the need for teachers. He felt that though these teachers might be less qualified in terms of formal teacher training, because of their religious convictions they would work for less wages and thus save the government funds.

Prime Minister John A. Macdonald concurred with the Davin Report even though he believed that a secular foundation for public education was the best approach. When it came to the First Nations, however, he was of the opinion that the primary objective should be to help them become "civilized" men and women and this could best be achieved through religious instruction. Residential schools could function to achieve this goal in two ways; first, they would remove Aboriginal children from the negative influences of their parents, and second, church-trained teachers could teach the children Christian virtues (Miller, 1997: 103).

The Laurier Liberal government succeeded the Macdonald Tories and Clifford Sifton, Minister of the Interior, automatically became General Superintendent of Indian Affairs. This was the practice of the time. In 1936 the Indian Affairs Department was transferred from the Department of the Interior to the Department of Mines and Resources. In 1950 it was shifted to the Department of Citizenship and Immigration and then in 1966 the Department of Indian Affairs and Northern Development was established. In any event, Sifton carried on the tradition of funding Indian schools and letting church denominations run them. Unfortunately, he also transferred the office of Commissioner of Indian Affairs from Regina to Ottawa, leaving the management of residential schools entirely in the hands of local administrators.

Sifton first appointed Frank Pedley as Deputy Superintendent General, and Pedley was followed by Duncan Campbell Scott who held that office from 1913 to 1932. Scott was a true imperialist who believed that the British Empire was God's gift to mankind. It was his strong conviction that education would be the key by which to bring the First Nations into the 20th century. He entrusted this and other responsibilities to nonNative Indian agents whom he assigned to reserves and they were expected to obey his edicts. Although religious orders were in charge of schooling, they were expected to work hand in hand with the local Indian agent.

During both Macdonald and Laurier's reign, the campaign to make-over Indians became more pronounced. The arena of schooling was the obvious target, highlighted with the operation of a series of residential schools spread across the continent, aimed at turning Indian children into clones of European culture. The formal residential school period began in 1868 and ended in the 1980s. There is some disagreement among historians about exact closing dates since some residential schools were operated by local bands for a few years before their final closure.

A number of pre-20th century developments contributed to the ongoing problematic conditions of First Nations' education, primarily the signing of treaties and the development of the reserve system. The latter brought about permanent settlements for the Indian. With the demise of the buffalo by the mid 1880s, a radical shift in the Indian economy became a necessity. In the west, for example, it was expected that the buffalo economy would last until well into the 1890s but events moved too quickly. Even before the 20th century rang in, starvation and economic devastation were widespread among Plains Indians (Wuttunee, 1971; Dempsey, 1978).

Twentieth Century Developments

The first half of this century featured a fairly common pattern for Native education in Canada. Missionaries went about the work of "Christianizing, educating and civilizing," and generally trying to stir up enthusiasm for their cause among Indian parents and their children. Aboriginal parents were concerned about the loss of their culture through the assimilative efforts of federally-sponsored mission schools, and reacted strongly to what they perceived as a campaign to malign and denigrate their culture. They successfully sought to frustrate missionary efforts in the form of a high rate of absenteeism with the result that very few Aboriginal children graduated from elementary school.

The post-treaty era of 1921-1940 saw the perpetuation of the same assimilationist educational policy in Canadian Native education. Gradually government officials encouraged school administrators to continue to enroll Aboriginal children in their schools so that school enrollment figures rose from 3 000 in 1930 to 118 000 by 1940. Residential schools had a side benefit in that the arrangement made it easier to deal with health problems. For example, in 1936 when tuberculosis was virtually out of control, children in federal schools were targeted for health care while the rest of the Indian population could not be reached. Reports on Indian progress were mixed, ranging from outright condemnation to modest hope that the Aboriginals would valiantly bear the ordeal of contact with advanced European civilization. The next decade continued much in the same vein except that Indian people gradually began to organize and speak out against conditions regarding reserve education. Government reaction was to transfer administrative authority of Indian schools from religious organizations to the Federal Department of Indian Affairs and parallelled this action by phasing out residential schools.

Despite the best efforts of residential school educators, the two societal domains, Native and nonNative, continued to operate independently of one another. Aboriginal students who endured the system through the years to their time of leaving, in most cases still found it impossible to adjust to the outside social order. Moreover, they were often ill-equipped to deal with their own communities when they returned to them. In order to survive they formulated an artificial self when conditions required them to deal with both worlds simultaneously.

By the 1940s the handwriting was on the wall; the residential schools were not accomplishing what they were designed to do. In 1947 the shift in government policy was mandated in a paper entitled, "A plan to liquidate Canada's Indian problem in twenty-five years" (Pauls, 1984: 33). The scheme outlined a plan to transfer authority for the operation of Indian schools from federal to provincial governments, a stance which was later reiterated in the White Paper of 1969. Integration, rather than assimilation, was envisaged as the basis of the new policy except that it was to be one-way. First Nations students would interact with their nonNative peers who would influence Indian students with their dominant societal values. In the final analysis, Aboriginal children were still expected to absorb the values of European culture (Allison, 1983: 119). The "Indian problem" remained unresolved, and the economic gap between Aboriginal peoples and other Canadians had not been eliminated. Before another line of attack was devised, however, plans were made to turn over administration of residential schools directly into the hands of government bureaucrats instead of religious leaders.

The process of transferring administration of residential schools to secular control began in 1949. That year a Special Joint Committee of the Senate and the House of Commons recommended that wherever possible Indian children should be educated in integrated schools. The bottom line was that education following the traditional European format was still perceived as the vehicle by which the assimilation of First Nations could come about (Hawthorn, 1967). At most Aboriginal parents would be invited to sit on advisory boards, but not have an official voice in determining either educational policy-making or school procedure. Integration in this mode was to be the order of the day. By 1970, Indian opposition peaked, and the Indigenous people made it clear that they were serious about wanting to control the education of their children. This determination continues to this day. Successive, minor changes in government attitude have illustrated that such a format will indicate a significant directional change for Canada's First Nations. In the meantime, it will be difficult for Aboriginal People to offset the inertia of several centuries of attempted assimilationist thrusts forced at them by sometimes well-meaning pedagogues backed by government funds and policies.

The decline of residential schools began in the 1950s, basically at the time that the government began to increase its involvement in Native education (King, 1967: 87). Administrative control of the schools was taken away from religious bodies and assigned to civil servants. Simultaneously, in line with the North American Indian renaissance movement which motivated many First Nations to question government policies (Lincoln, 1985), Aboriginal parents began protesting school operations. It took more than a century of resistance to religious and cultural indoctrination before First Nations forcefully expressed that they were very unhappy with the arrangement. One of the primary arms of the cultural renaissance movement was to try to halt the assimilationist thrust of the school. Since then the campaign has increasingly been fortified by an ever intensifying spiritual and cultural resurgence of traditional ways. The magnitude of this movement is difficult for outsiders to comprehend or assess, but its future impact is unmistakable and easy to underestimate.

When the Native resistance movement first began its principal speakers were often Aboriginals who had been educated in residential schools and who knew first-hand what they were talking about. In 1970, following a successful experiment in local control on the Navajo Reservation at Rough Rock, Arizona, a group of protesting Aboriginal parents at St. Paul, Alberta, took charge of their own school. This event significantly changed the face of Native education in Canada.

Life in Residential Schools

To begin with, occupants living in a residential school of necessity had to cope within a highly structured form of institutional life. Church-employed staff constituted the power structure and the ideological ethos of the school. Since their identity was theologically-derived (European style), it was inevitable that their view was to be regarded as having a higher authority than that of parents or students. The status of religious leaders was different than that of hired teachers, since these leaders made the rules. Even then, there was often disagreement about how children should be treated and how schools should be run. As King has pointed out (1967: 58), many teachers who worked in residential schools were ill-qualified to do so. Often they had only recently immigrated to Canada, and did not fully understand Canada's history or value system. Even more importantly, they knew little or nothing about the First Nations' way of life. At best they were only minimally-educated and came from lower socio-economic backgrounds, but they were armed with a strong sense of mission. If their mission was frustrated in any sense, the natural outlet for personal aggression was to target the children. Teachers also discovered that personnel in the upper administrative echelons were virtually inflexible and unmovable.

In residential schools the relationship between students and adults was basically set in a fixed mode of power structure. Students were forced to see adults as controllers of their fate. Because the children often did not know what the precise rules dictated (and there were rules about everything), students appeared to be uncertain and easily directed. No doubt this kind of socialization pattern greatly affected the students' decision-making abilities in later life. Grant (1996: 89) argues that the intent of residential school education was never to fully educate Indian youngsters because if they were too well prepared they would become a threat to dominant society. Barman (1986) supports this observation and suggests that nonNative Canadians never wanted young Aboriginals to enter their socio-economic order, even at the bottom rung because they feared the Indigenous people might be successful. This implies that if Indian youth triumphed by surviving residential school, they would face additional road-blocks and discrimination ahead. The bottom line was that Indian children were imprisoned on the pretext of educating them, while in reality their potential to develop fully as members of either Native or nonNative society was squelched.

Daily Schedules

Daily activities in a residential school were quite crude and very public. Initially the huge brick buildings had sealed windows which often produced a foul smell or rank odor, and no doubt contributed towards the spread of diseases. Grant (1996: 123) cites one school in which 26 of the boys were bedwetters. When it was discovered that fresh air might be a solution to dormitory odors, the other extreme was practiced and the windows were left open at night. Thus the children often slept in what seemed like freezer compartments because of frigid air invading their rooms.

Bathing was done in groups, with the younger students bathing first. The water was often too hot when they started the ritual, but by the time the older students got their turn the water was cold and dirty. Calloway (1996: 14) notes that when the children arrived at residential school they were given new names to replace their traditional ones, stiff uniforms in place of their Native clothing, and haircuts. As if cutting the hair was not a sufficient form of insult to cultural adherents who revered long hair, students who ran away had their hair completely shorn. As one young female student put it:

> When I got back to school, because I ran away, they were going to give me punishment. So instead of strapping me, they said, "You got to kneel down on the floor, in front of everybody, and tell them you're sorry you ran away. . . ." Because I ran away, they said they were going to give me a real short haircut for my punishment. So my hair was cut really short, almost like a boy's. (Alice in Haig-Brown, 1993: 84)

Quality of food consumed was a common complaint with many former residents recalling long periods of time when they went hungry. Some students were driven to steal bread from the kitchen, but if they were caught their punishment was severe. Haig-Brown (1993: 99) indicates that sharing stolen food resulted in the development of a unique subculture. Stealing food was such a complex operation that it involved a number of participants, some to serve as look-out guards, others to engage in the act of stealing, and still others to distribute the goods.

In most schools, the staff ate better food than the children although there were exceptions. Food supplies were limited and portions were small. If the prospect of a second helping was feasible, students would wolf down their food as fast as possible in hopes of getting an additional helping. Later on parents were often aghast when they discovered the undisciplined eating habits of their offspring. Once downed, the food was seldom allowed to digest naturally for the condition of the children's bowels was another staff concern. Part of the daily routine was to administer a laxative to the children, many of whom really did not need it. Often the number of toilet pails provided was insufficient for the need. At times students would dare to use a nearby staff bathroom only to run the risk of being caught and severely punished.

On entering the residential school children were issued an annual supply of clothing and told they would get no additional items until the following year. If the youth outgrew certain items like shoes, or if the holes in them got too large, it was the students' problem. There were no additional issues. This policy seemed to apply to other areas as well, for example in the issuance of medical supplies. Many nuns and teachers were not trained in the area of health education, and they disdained the use of Aboriginal remedies, so they were ill-equipped to help when the children got sick. Unless hospital facilities were close by, children were treated in the school, a situation which often led to the spread of the illness. Extensive illnesses also led to death, although no one ever talked about this in the schools. Grant (1996: 133) reports that in 1928 in one school, 15 percent of the students died.

School Content

The curriculum of residential schools was primarily based on the four "R's"– readin', 'ritin' and 'rithmetic – plus large doses of religious instruction. Perley (1993: 123) notes that the latter was indubitably the most important of the four components. The range of subjects taught generally included reading, writing, grammar, composition, and art with specialized subjects such as farming and trades (blacksmithing) for boys. Girls were taught housekeeping, mending, knitting, and fancy work. Rote was a valued form of learning and students spent endless hours learning to feed-back the desired bits of knowledge. The flip-side of learning was to dismantle the children of any traditional Aboriginal ideas and concept they might be harboring in their minds. The use of Aboriginal languages was discouraged and students were severely punished if they were caught speaking their mother tongues. There were never any references made at any time to the history or cultures of First Nations. These were completely ignored. Music and songs taught reflected only the themes of English and French societies, and later on those of the new dominant society. Academic achievement was low, based partially on the fact that teachers had low expectations of students and many teachers were ill-prepared to teach. When students later transferred to provincial schools for high school training they were often ashamed of their poor records. Truly the basis of the system was inadequate, demeaning, and dehumanizing, as may be substantiated by the practice in some schools of referring to students only by their assigned numbers instead of using their names. Small wonder that less than three percent of those children attending residential schools ever graduated from high school.

The question often arises, "Why did Indigenous parents even consider enrolling their children in such a dreadful environment?" The answer is not singularly dimensional because the publicity about residential schools was not always straightforward. In Canada, for the most part, parents did not have a choice. Members of the Royal Canadian Mounted Police came to their homes and took the children away. There were some parents who sent their children to residential schools because they believed that the schools were the "only way to salvation," having been given such information by religious personnel. Other parents, who were having a difficult time supporting their families because of changing economic conditions grudgingly released their children with the hopes that they would have a better chance because of the promised enhanced skills they would learn in school. Ellis (1996: 779) suggests that some parents gave up their children in order to gain points with the local Indian agent; by coming on side with his recommendations they hoped to be more favorably done by in terms of gaining needed supplies.

Despite the grievous nature of happenings in the residential milieu a small number of former residential dwellers managed to hold onto a workable form of self-esteem and today they are able to communicate effectively about the current needs in First Nations' education. Perhaps they learned too well, what was being taught so that government and church leaders got more than they bargained for. These individuals are now able clearly to articulate in language which bureaucrats can understand how to compensate for the years of cruelty and neglect which First Nations in Canada have suffered at their hands.

Grant (1996) catalogues the negative results of the residential school phenomenon to include an inability to express feelings, apathy and unwillingness to work, values confusion and culture shock, anti-religious attitudes, and long-term negative impact on succeeding generations. Many former inmates, unable to rid themselves of the unhappy tendencies which they witnessed and experienced at the hands of the staff and teachers, by modelling simply passed them on to their children. Their behavior in parenting much resembled that of their own caregivers in residential schools.

When the residential schools began closing down, a number of them were modified to suit other purposes. Several of them were managed for a few years by committees and school boards established by First Nations themselves. In 1995, for example, six residential schools in Saskatchewan were operating under Native management. Several former residential schools that were not demolished were converted into cultural centres, adult learning centres, or private schools, but many were simply demolished. When the administration of these schools was transferred to Native control, the influence of Indian input was quickly evident. Gradually, First Nations' influence had won out over past EuroCanadian domination. For example, when the final closing exercises of several residential schools transpired in the 1980s (for example, Qu'Appelle Indian Residential School in Saskatchewan), Native dancing and social events took precedence over denominational activities (Gresko, 1986: 89).

The largest residential school on the prairies was located at Lebret, Saskatchewan, and enrolled 350 children. At community request it was demolished in 1999. As a local Aboriginal resident stated to the author, "It's not so much a matter of anticipated extensive expenses to keep the building going; the school has too many bad memories to remain standing."

The Aftermath

Researchers in Canada have identified three separate stages of Indian education prior to the First Nations' takeover of their schools (Haig-Brown, 1993). From about 1930 to 1945 religious denominations worked hand in hand with government in promoting education to keep Aboriginal children apart from dominant society in residential or day schools. The overarching atmosphere in these schools was paternalistic, protectionist, and isolationist. Then things changed, and from 1945 to 1960, partially due to protests from Aboriginal parents, governments bureaucrats began to involve themselves increasingly in the operation of these schools (Littlebear, 1992). This was the second stage.

The third stage witnessed increased concern on the part of Indian parents who observed that the emphases of school curricula and program content were depriving their children of their cultural heritage and identity. They were devastated by the 94 percent drop-out rate of Indian students in Canada and bemoaned the lack of adequate role models. Their educational objectives for their children were sometimes phrased in this manner:

> Our aim is to affect a true sense of identity for ourselves by recognizing traditional values while simultaneously preparing ourselves to function effectively in the larger society. (Haig-Brown, 1993: 132)

When the residential school system was finally shut down, it did not signal an end to the ongoing struggle for cultural recognition and meaningful education for Native people. They still faced the perpetual challenge of not yielding to the subtle influence of assimilation. Assimilation takes on quite subversive forms. Even today, as the trend towards increasing involvement in local schooling on the part of First Nations continues, observers have to note with caution that it is a step on the right direction. However, those who are more optimistic believe that local governance of this institution will reinforce the needed components of cultural awareness and enhanced self-esteem, and lend political energy to the First Nations' campaign to reestablish themselves in the 21st century on this continent on their own terms.

Residential School Litigations

The residential school phenomenon will not go away. While only about 20 percent of First Nations children ever attended residential schools, many of them and/or their descendants are claiming sexual and/or physical abuse or cultural loss as a result of the experience. There are more than 6 000 cases before the courts, naming church denominations as well as government in their litigations. Anglican, Presbyterian, Roman Catholic, and United Churches now face significant costs which could bankrupt them if the Indian people are successful (Copley, 2002; Frank, 2000; Outerbridge, 2000; Wilson, 2000; Woodward, 2000).

So far the Anglican Church has been hit hardest by residential school litigations, shelling out as much as one hundred thousand dollars a month in legal fees. Their total costs to date for nine dioceses for this purpose have passed five million dollars, but observers suspect that only one percent of the winnings ever reaches the plaintiffs. One party found guilty is the Diocese of Cariboo in southeastern British Columbia which declared bankruptcy in 2001. The move affected 17 Anglican congregations in British Columbia's interior valley region (Copley, 2002: 31).

The resolution of residential school court cases is not always what it might appear to be. For example, on July 12, 2001, the Supreme Court of British Columbia authorized an award of half a million dollars to a group of six Aboriginal litigants for damages suffered because of their residential school experiences. Originally the group had asked for five million dollars, but when the bills were settled, it appeared doubtful that the litigants would receive any of the money. Their lawyers deducted 40 percent for their expenses, and when court costs were calculated, the prosecutors would "hardly see a dime of the awards" (*Calgary Herald*, April 14, 2001). The court ruled that in this case United Church of Canada was 25 percent responsible for these crimes and the federal government was 75 percent responsible.

In an unexpected development, in December 2001, British Columbia Supreme Court Justice Bruce Cohen awarded an Aboriginal man identified only as EB the sum of $200 000 for sexual abuse he suffered as an eight-year old in the Christie Residential School on Meares Island. It was the highest award for such a case in the province's history. Christie Residential School was run by the Oblates and the offender, now deceased, had a previous murder conviction before he started working at the school as a baker. Central to the case was the claim that the church should have done a background check before hiring the man. Brian Savage of *The Alberta Native News* (January 2002: 7) quoted Chief Robert Joseph,

It's quite common to discover that the pedophiles who reigned throughout these schools moved from school to school. It's a clear pattern and there should have been a much more stringent background check of employees to make sure that young children were protected.

The encouraging results of this settlement could motivate many more. The number of cases before the courts could go as high as 15 000 or more since many as many as 90 000 children attended residential schools throughout the years that the system operated. The Oblates have appealed the decision of the British Columbia Supreme Court and are demanding that EB pay for their court costs.

Student Memories

In addition to laying claim to settlement funds for physical and sexual abuse, some Aboriginals are asking for damages pertaining to loss of language and culture (Hookimaw-Witt, 1998). The federal government seems reluctant to bargain in that area, choosing to define the issues in narrow terms. If interpreted on a wider scale, individual damages could go well beyond the parameters of residential school cases. However, court settlements, financial awards, and sometimes even personal counselling cannot eliminate the painful tragedy of young lives having been spoiled by preying perverts in the past. The following personal quotations give testimony to this sad fact.

> The "Graduates" of the "Ste. Anne's Residential School" era are now trying and often failing to come to grips with life as adults after being treated as children in an atmosphere of fear, loneliness and loathing. (Albany Chief in Milloy, 1999: 295)

> It will be difficult for many of us to talk about our experiences and how they affected our lives after we left the schools because of the simple fact that they bring back too many painful and unhappy memories. (Chief Bev Sellers in Furniss, 1995: 121)

> I was frustrated about how we were treated, humiliated, and degraded, so I drank and took drugs to numb the frustrations of how my life had turned out. (A. Collison to L. Jaine in Hare and Barman, 2000: 342)

> I've lost a lot of friends. A quarter of them are dead, they couldn't stand it. They put me through seven years of hell for no reason – just because I was a Roman Catholic Indian. (Philip Michel in Grant, 1996: 247)

But that is one of the things I want to stress; the lonely part of residential school life. The other things you can live through, like the food and the bad clothing and stuff like that. That's minor. But when it has to do with feelings. That was something that I thought would never heal. I understand. I got through that a few years ago. (Dan Keshane in Miller, 1997: 342)

Hugs were something I never experienced in school. (Chief Phil Fontaine in Miller, 1997: 339)

Sometimes I get scared–scared for the children. Language takes my children away from me, that is why I am scared. They do not hear my words. When he throws his language away, that is when it starts. He makes fun of his father and mother, his grandfather and grandmother. (Alex Bonais in Ing, 1991: 81)

Despite these unfortunate experiences, the vitality and strength of the Aboriginal worldview is affirmed in the following testimony:

In retrospect there are times when I thank them [residential school teachers] ... because they put fight into me physically and mentally ... and having survived that, I think I can survive anything. (Charlie in Haig-Brown, 1993: 116)

The physical, mental, and spiritual strength inherent in this last quotation could the spark by which to ignite a forest fire of a renewed Indigenous renaissance (Miller, 1987). Hopefully, nonNative Canadians will be sufficiently alert to heed it and work in tandem with Indigenous people to help them recover and build for the future.

Seven

Métis Education in Canada

To a great extent education will be the key that allows Métis people to enter the mainstream of society and operate within it as equals. The Métis, as a group, have chosen complete integration despite the difficulty in achieving it. Their official organization recognizes progress in education as the factor most likely to assist in achieving that objective. (Sealey and Lussier, 1975: 179)

Even if the pessimistic becomes reality, there is one thing Canadians should have learned in the last hundred years–the Métis will not abandon their struggle. If a satisfactory accommodation is not reached in the next few years, in two of three decades the struggle will regain its momentum. (Purich, 1988: 194)

Aboriginal literature and creative arts need to be expanded and infused with their unique Indigenous vision . . . .At present there is a renaissance among self-conscious artists, authors, poets, and intellectuals who hold strong national and class beliefs. . . . The Indian/Métis consciousness and culture-building of today is stronger and more significant than ever in our history. (Adams, 1999: 115)

Our Mission is to provide, in partnership with parents and community, high quality education for all students so that they can develop the skills, knowledge, attitudes, and character essential for successful participation in our changing society. (Frontier School Division No. 48, Province of Manitoba, 2000)

Since the larger Native Canadian community includes a fair range of legal identities – Status-Treaty, Status-nonTreaty, nonStatus, Inuit, and Métis, it seems only logical to include a narrative regarding the latter group. According to the historical record, the Métis have figured as a separate entity since at least 1869 when the formation of the Province of Manitoba was in process. In addition, their educational saga comprises a unique chapter in Canadian history (Friesen, 1996).

For several decades the Manitoba Métis Federation has promoted the concept that economic success and psychological well-being for Métis people will best be accomplished through improved education. The subtle truth assumption behind this approach, however, is assimilation, but that objective is continually being reassessed by the newer generations of Métis. The happy end result, hopefully, will be a reconciliation of the longstanding federal education policy of assimilation with the campaign for self-determination fostered by most Native communities today (Tobias, 1988; 154; Brookes, 1991).

The first half of the 20th century did not belong to the Métis. Unlike Treaty Indians they did not have any kind of legal status nor designated lands to occupy. Of course the establishment of reserves did little to advance Indian development per se since the First Nations were still dependent upon government for rations for long periods of time. In the eyes of the Métis, however, Status Indians at least had a land base.

The educational history of the Métis at the turn of the last century correlated with the span of their economic involvements. After the defeat of Louis Riel in 1885, the Métis basically gravitated toward one of three routes. *First,* there were those who opted for the more traditional Native way of life whose communities became targets of missionary education. Métis children too were educated in Indian day schools and later residential schools. *Second,* there were those who migrated west of Manitoba and engaged in various limited or seasonal job markets. Their children got potluck by way of education. *Third,* those who tried to integrate into the society of the incoming Europeans and so were educated in Canada's slowly developing school system.

The educational attainments of the Métis who joined with Aboriginal tribes were dependent upon developments on the Indian reserves. When there was room in reserve schools, Métis children who lived in nearby communities were allowed to attend. Although their parents were not permitted by law to live on the reserve, they basically adopted a reserve type of life. Because of this the Métis needed the same services in education, health, and welfare as Status Indians, but they were not served in this respect by the Indian Affairs Branch of the federal government. Since the provinces were slow to respond to nonStatus needs this segment of Métis fared even worse than their Indian counterparts (Sealey and Lussier, 1975: 147).

The contingent of Métis who opted for life further west after the Riel defeat often found themselves occupying quickly-constructed shantytowns located at the edge of EuroCanadian towns, but these settlements quickly deteriorated into Canada's first 20th century slums. The odds were against them, and in the words of Maria Campbell, "So began a miserable life of poverty which held no hope for the future. That generation of my people was completely beaten" (Campbell, 1973: 13).

Western Canadian Métis settlements were unusually stable in nature, unlike the towns near which they were situated. The vocations they pursued included agriculture and fishing, and many of the men worked for the railway or in lumber camps or sawmills. Schools in the settlements were mainly established by church denominations, but a lack of funds allowed most of the schools to operate only a few months each year. Thus each succeeding generation of Métis tended to have less schooling than the previous (Sealey, 1980: 38). Many of the Métis settlements endured well past the midpoint of the 20th century probably basing their durability upon hard work and a variety of secondary factors.

The Métis who adapted most successfully, from an economic point of view, were those who opted for integration into the dominant EuroCanadian culture. Most of them gave up or denied their Aboriginal roots and strove to be accepted by and be successful at jobs approved by the Canadian majority (Giraud, 1956). The late Howard Adams, a Native activist and for many years a professor at the University of Saskatchewan, admitted that his own academic and social successes came at the expense of abandoning his Native ancestry and connections. Suddenly, in 1948, when his 52 year-old mother died, he realized that what he had perceived as a cultural albatross really constituted the essence of his very being. (Adams, 1975: 41-43). Was all the denial worth it? According to Adams it was not – not with the continual reminder that he had knowingly abandoned his heritage.

Evidently the assimilation process was very effective with the Métis people. According to the 1941 census there were only 26 660 Métis in Canada – 8 692 in Manitoba, 8 808 in Alberta, and 9 160 in Saskatchewan (Sealey and Lussier, 1975: 140). This compares, for example, with an earlier figure of 10 398 resident Métis in Manitoba in 1870 (Lusty, 1973: 10).

It would be incorrect to suggest that the deplorable educational conditions among northern Métis were always ignored by government. At first the federal government accepted the responsibility of providing schooling for all persons of Native ancestry following Davin's recommendations in 1879. Davin's report focussed on the northwest but excluded Manitoba. Davin urged that both Status Indians and mixed-bloods be educated in order to provide them with the skills needed to assure them a better future. In 1932, L'Association des Métis de l'Alberta (which later became the Métis Association of Alberta), was formed to draw the government's attention to the plight of the Métis of that province (MacEwan, 1981: 141). Also in 1932, Charles Parker, Inspector for the Indian Agencies in the Mackenzie District, urged that government leaders pay heed to the unfortunate living conditions among the half-breeds of the north. He saw the Métis as poor outcasts, victims of one of the most iniquitous schemes ever fostered and maliciously operated, who should be awarded the full privileges of Status Indians. Ten years later, some Métis in the Mackenzie District were added to the respective treaty list on the basis that they were economically much worse off than Status Indians. Even then, coupled with other parallel efforts the future of the Métis depended on the collective will and determination of the people themselves to find solutions and bring about needed change (Fumoleau, 1973: 272).

In evaluating Canadian Indian and Métis education in the last century it is helpful to maintain a national perspective of happenings across the nation. Public education was generally non-existent in the west at the beginning of the 20th century, although Manitoba passed a School Attendance Act in 1916, which made school attendance compulsory for children ages 5 to 14. David J. Goggin, Superintendent of Education for the Northwest Territories (which at that time included Alberta and Saskatchewan), engineered the formulation of a public system of education during his years of office from 1883 to 1912. Previous to this public education in Canada had adopted certain distinguishable marks and wrestled with the issues of organization, philosophy, and financing (Patterson, Chalmers and Friesen, 1974: 98). Most of the advances in education hardly affected the Native population except for those Métis who chose to enter the Canadian mainstream through integration or assimilation.

An evaluation of schooling in Manitoba in 1938 revealed that most schools operating in Native communities were under religious jurisdiction and their teachers had inadequate training. Much of the curriculum emphasis was on religion to the detriment of the academic subjects (Sealey, 1980: 34). A parallel development was the "orphan school" developed by C. K. Rogers, a senior administrator with the Department of Education in Manitoba from 1928 to 1959. Each spring, any surplus money from a supply budget was put into a special fund and used to send teachers to remote areas to teach in the orphan schools. Those participating included unemployed teachers and university students. No school buildings were available to the teachers so a variety of other facilities were used. The curriculum offered minimal instruction in the three "R's," no inspectors visited the schools, and apparently no records were kept. The orphan schools were closed after World War II when the province was able to finance the extension of its public system further north (Sealey, 1980: 45).

The road to universal public education in the northern regions of the prairie provinces was often fraught with complex conditions. During the 1940s, unless the churches provided them, many northern districts did not even have schools. As late as the early 1960s there were still many mission schools operating across the prairie provinces. This situation prevailed partially because of the difficulty in establishing a public system. In Alberta, for example, there were three requirements for the establishment of a school district including: (i) at least eight school-age children had to be resident in the proposed district; (ii) enough assessable, deeded land had to be registered to provide a tax base to raise the necessary revenue; and, (iii) the consent of the majority of taxpayers in said district had to be rendered. The second criterion was the most difficult to meet because much northern occupied land was not owned by individuals and therefore could not be taxed. As a result residents were neither owners nor electors and they could not have established a school district if they had wanted to (Chalmers, 1977).

Toward Formal School Systems

Saskatchewan

After the Second World War many social changes in Canada came about, particularly in regard to education. In 1939, Saskatchewan's N. L. Reid of the province's Department of Education surveyed the educational situation of the province's northern regions but his report was filed and forgotten until after the war. Another study, conducted five years later, suggested the establishment of a special northern school district to meet the needs of northern dwellers, particularly the Métis. The task was ultimately undertaken and although local advisory groups were arranged for, administrative power lay with the Northern Education Committee which was responsible to the Minister of Education.

Very early in the operation of the new school board it was reported that additional school buildings and teacher residences had been built and equipped, and old ones repaired. Better qualified teachers were hired and the pupil enrollment more than doubled (Knill and Davies, 1966: 202). Another base for later developments was a proposal in 1959, by Métis leader Jim Brady, on behalf of the Lac La Ronge School District in which he laid out a series of major proposals for educational development in the north including: (i) equality of education for Native people, even if costs were high; (ii) rigorous enforcement of compulsory education among Native peoples; (iii) educational training for citizenship including instruction in student self-government; (iv) adult education courses for basic literacy; and, (v) the establishment of a special selection apparatus for northern teaching appointments (Dobbin, 1981: 208).

More than a decade passed before Brady's suggestions were examined. Finally, in 1972, the Saskatchewan provincial government created the

Department of Northern Saskatchewan with a branch Northern School Board, presently known as Northern Lights School Division No. 113. The responsibility of the division is solely in the area of Native education and in its initial efforts this body managed to improve transportation facilities and health services and formulate effective conservation policies. The government acted on the basis of three previously-approved objectives: (i) to give all northern children the best possible educational opportunities; (ii) to extend the educational program into the community by encouraging local participation and responsibility; and, (iii) to encourage residents of communities to accept increasing responsibility for the operation of their schools (Knill and Davies, 1966: 287-288).

At present the Northern Lights School Division is committed to serving Cree, Dene, Métis, and EuroCanadian cultures and operates 26 schools with student populations ranging from 12 to 500 students per school. Division administrators insist they are progressively piloting programs unique to Canada, by staying on the cutting edge of technology, and integrating the cultural aspects of the varied communities they serve in the classrooms.

Alberta

In the later 1950s, school administrators in Alberta who were responsible for managing federal schools found that they had a shortage of space and simply could not accommodate nonStatus or Métis children in their schools. These children were after all the responsibility of the Provincial Department of Education. Established independent northern school districts were also clamoring for space and denominational schools were struggling with a usual shortage of funds. With federal encouragement, administrators who were aware that they did not legally have to accommodate nonStatus students in their schools, approached the province to assume their legal responsibility. Yielding to legal logic, the province assigned the responsibility for educating Métis children over to the provincial Department of Education. The previous practice, albeit not completely satisfactory, was that the federal government charged the provincial government a tuition fee for each nonStatus or Métis student enrolled in their schools.

Soon additional provincial school districts were designed in northern Alberta, for example, at Grouard, Wabasca, and Trout Lake, for a total of 20 districts in operation by the fall of 1960s (Chalmers, 1984: 5). By the end of the year, on December 30, 1960, the province had established the Northland School Division under the leadership of a three-person board. The new district also took in the Métis colony schools with the exception of Paddle Prairie which joined the Fort Vermilion School Division. The innovative

Northland system included a student body of over 2 300 children whose previous school experiences included mission, Indian, public and Métis colony schools. According to Chalmers' definition of "Métis," almost half of the student body (1 265 students) were Métis (Ledgerwood, 1972: 16).

The Northland School Division began with a very simple administrative structure and operated according to a flexible policy. No one was permitted to refer to the previous year's minutes in resolving problems. Moreover, the government gave administrators a freer hand in finances; funds, once granted to Northland, could not be recalled nor re-allocated to any other educational activity. Observers called the Northland Division the "Moose Division" because it was "big, awkward and went like hell" (Chalmers, 1977).

In 1961, the federal and provincial governments signed an agreement to build vocational schools in northern districts on a shared cost basis. The Northland School Division opened such a school in Grouard and accepted students who were in grades eight or nine, but maintained its primary objective of job training. It was hoped that school graduates would be able to obtain jobs in northern Native settlements so that they would not find it necessary to relocate to larger, more southerly centres. By 1963, other school districts further south adopted this practice as well and discovered that the program attracted many non-academic nonNative students as well (Chalmers, 1967: 278-279). This format of education was initiated on the platform of educational integration which was seen as an irreversible and effective process. As discussed earlier, educational integration was simultaneously being promulgated in First Nations' communities.

In 1965, the Province of Alberta passed an act of legislation specifically for the Northland School Division to be managed by a government-appointed board. Initially reports were that the new school division started off on a solid base but within a decade there were rumblings of concern and discontent. Administrators and legislators worked hard to alleviate arising tensions and despite rough times, succeeded in developing a workable northern school division. Today, the Northland School Division is managed by ten staff administrators servicing 23 schools in an area highlighted by five major water systems, covering a 250 000 square metre area.

Manitoba

Following the example of the two more westerly provinces, Manitoba eventually addressed the subject of Métis education as well. Earlier, in 1947, a special committee had been appointed by the Manitoba government to enquire into Hutterite education. The supervisor of the project energetically travelled the northern regions of the province, through remote communities, evaluating educational conditions. After completing their evaluation the committee report urged rapid action, and the government quickly responded. In 1957 the Supervisor of Special Schools was assigned 35 schools comprising a total of 100 classrooms of students (Sealey, 1980: 47). Two years later a report was issued by the provincial Social and Economic Research Office on behalf of the Department of Agriculture and Immigration regarding the living conditions of the Manitoba population of Indian ancestry. In examining the special school situation the framers of the report indicated that the supervisor had too heavy a workload which should be readjusted and more supervisory staff should be hired. It was also reported that the most significant achievement in terms of Métis education was the fact that children were attending school in larger numbers than in the previous years. However, the dropout rate was still very high and the average leaving grade was 5.84 (Lagasse, 1959, Vol. 1: 128).

The report completed by the Department of Agriculture and Immigration encompassed three volumes and surveyed Métis people from a variety of life situations. Surveyors examined the living conditions of Métis communities situated on the fringe of Indian reserves, those living on the edges of nonNative settlements, and those living in predominantly Métis communities. They also spent time in Métis settlements near predominantly EuroCanadian communities and those which were not accessible by roads along the northern railway lines. The researchers estimated that 80 percent of Manitoba's Métis were not included in the study because they would already have integrated into dominant society to the point of not being recognized as even having Native heritage (Lagasse, 1959, Vol. 1: 77).

A number of concerns emanated from the Manitoba report, particularly the high dropout rate of Métis students. Reasons for leaving school were not surprising, and students who were surveyed included these reasons for leaving school: had to go to work, had to stay home and help, got tired of school or did not like school, further schooling not available, could not afford to go, had an illness. (Lagasse, 1959, Vol. II: 53-56). Five factors were identified that hindered Métis education and the Department of Education was urged to rectify them. These included: (i) education could not be delivered to isolated communities situated too far away from accessible roadways; (ii) age-grade retardation; (iii) lack of attendance related to age-grade retardation; (iv) administration and supervision problems; and, (v) the need for remedial services (Lagasse, 1959, Vol. III: 121).

The Manitoba report concluded with a number of significant recommendations urging improved school facilities, better qualified teachers, enhanced financing, stronger measures of enforcement for school attendance, and the provision of remedial services. The report recommended that more permanent kinds of job opportunities for Métis breadwinners would discourage the nomadic way of life and encourage improved school attendance on the part of the children. Finally, the report encouraged an integrated form of education, mixing Métis with nonNative children in provincial schools so that the attitudes and morals of the EuroCanadian society would be more readily inculcated by Métis children (Lagasse, 1959, Vol. III: 132-133). This reflected the general trend in Native education policy fostered by the Federal Department of Indian Affairs Branch which, since 1949, had integrated education. The concept was that with this format, Native children would better be prepared to take their places as full-fledged Canadian citizens. (Brookes, 1991: 49-51). The federal government was adamant that "integration should not be confused, either in the minds of the Indian people, or the public at large, with assimilation" (Daniels, 1967: 28).

In 1963, a number of Manitoba's senior governmental officers and advisors travelled to northern Alberta to meet with the administration of the Northland School Division and visit some of the division's schools. They also studied the Saskatchewan arrangement and, in 1965, under Bill No. 47, created the Frontier School Division to operate under a single administrator. The initial aims of the new school division included: (i) the upgrading of school facilities and teacher accommodations; (ii) establishment of a high school to serve the needs of the constituency; and, (iii) improvement of instruction (Sealey and Kirkness, 1973: 143). Within five years the new Manitoba Division had hired 250 teachers to educate 5 000 students. The Division administration then purchased a former airforce base at Cranberry Portage, renovated it, and developed a residential high school. Thus, for the first time, Métis students in the northern and isolated regions of the province had available to them a secondary school with numerous options. In the first year the school attracted 189 students and by 1972 the enrollment was 701. Most of the students occupied dormitories at the Cranberry School, and others were billeted in private homes (Sealey, 1980: 49). This option again reflected the general Indian education policy adopted by the federal government through the Education Division of the Department of Indian Affairs, which tended to filter down in slightly modified form to provincial systems.

Problems and Complexities

The establishment of northern school systems in the Prairie Provinces did not immediately resolve all educational problems nor provide completely effective schooling to all areas. In many settlements the challenge of adequate education was primarily economic, not pedagogical. Many residents in the northern areas earned only meagre wages and often had to leave home for seasonal employment elsewhere. This necessity adversely affected family life. Researchers found that as self-sufficiency disappeared, so did the feeling of self-respect (Sealey and Lussier, 1975: 185). Education, if it was to be effective in this context, would have to incorporate the development of student self-esteem and social wellbeing. Many more ambitious individuals left their northern communities and migrated to more active northern centres or to larger towns and cities further south. However, unless those persons had the wherewithal to cope in urban settings, socially as well as in terms of the job market, they often found themselves lonely enough to want to return home accompanied by feelings of failure and without any prospects of employment on arrival home.

In 1972, the Manitoba Métis Federation prepared a document entitled, *In Search of a Future,* focussing attention on the challenges faced by Métis migrants in urban centres (Fulham, 1972). The report urged a government study to assess the economic viability of northern communities from where the migrants originated. The attainment of better education in isolated communities also implied the need for job placement after graduation. Another concern identified by the report was the adjustment process undergone by urban-migrating Métis, many of whom faced a complexity of personal problems after their relocation. The report also recommended the establishment of a series of migration centres to assist Métis in dealing with the challenges of relocation and job preparation (Sealey and Lussier, 1975: 187).

As though economic complications were not enough, the newly-developed northern prairie school systems soon encountered unforseen challenges which dampened the original enthusiasm of their promoters. This was amply demonstrated by development in the Northland School Division in Alberta. An evaluation of the Division a decade after its formulation revealed that while school enrollments had originally burgeoned, by the early 1970s the student population remained at a steady level. When the standards of achievement were compared with provincial schools, there was severe age-grade retardation, particularly at the primary levels. Although this retardation decreased dramatically in the initial decade, the dropout rate was still a cause for alarm. High school enrollment figures were low, and though even more students were enrolled in the upper grades, educators became concerned about the potentially dismal prospects faced by school graduates. Coupled with the fact of low employment opportunities in northern communities there was evidence that the school system was not adequately preparing students to face the limitations of the local job market or what to expect if they found it necessary to take up residence elsewhere.

In addition to pedagogical challenges, the Northland School Division had problems of an administrative nature as well. After a decade of "free spirit" operation, bureaucracy set in, and the flush of enthusiasm posited by the first administrators was replaced by management-oriented government bureaucrats who were more interested in setting budgets and cost-efficiency measures than pedagogy. These officials were anxious to hold the line on costs when they realized the enormity of expense connected to operating northern schools (Chalmers, 1972, 1977). It was also difficult to build up a stable teaching staff in Northland because of the remoteness of many of the schools and the undesirability of locating to these communities without relevant prior teaching experience. Teachers who did sign contracts with Northland encountered a variety of unexpected complications such as teaching a curriculum that was somewhat irrelevant, since it was geared to the EuroCanadian urban community, coping with teaching English as a second language, and learning how to survive in often isolated communities amidst extremely cold temperatures.

MacNeil Commission

In 1981, an Alberta provincial study undertaken by the MacNeil Commission identified a series of important problems for northern teachers. A primary concern was teacher turn-over, which sometimes reached up to 50 percent annually. The reasons teachers gave for disillusionment with northern teaching included a lack of preparation time, multi-grade classrooms, low levels of pupil achievement, and a number of factors connected with living in relatively isolated areas. A second concern identified by the Commission related to the view which Northland teachers had of the operations of the Northland School Division. Teachers felt that the board was not interested in developing good school-community relations and the board explicitly discouraged teachers from becoming too friendly with local residents. Generally, the Commission found that teacher morale was low and teachers felt that community perceptions of their profession were not very gratifying. They believed that their ideas were not really welcomed by the board and they feared punitive actions if they criticized the board or expressed dissatisfaction with working conditions (MacNeil, 1981: 31-32).

In 1981 a survey of local community residents in Fort Chipewyan, Alberta, one of the communities hosting a Northland Division school, revealed a number of problems connected to the local education milieu. The research work was carried out by a group of local citizens who were also enrolled in extension courses offered by the University of Calgary's Native Outreach Program. The study made note of several positive characteristics of the local schooling format, notably the fact that a local newspaper had been initiated by the school, traditional Native skills and crafts were being taught in the off-hours of school operation, and substitute teachers were being hired from among local citizens who had knowledge of local workings even if their educational qualifications were not up to provincial standards. This was especially appreciated by the teaching administration who had experienced difficulty in obtaining the assistance of substitute teachers in the past. Community residents were enthused about enhanced student achievement over the years that the Northland School had operated and expressed appreciation about the efforts of school staff who encouraged parent-community involvement (Friesen and Boberg, 1990: 151).

According to the study, Fort Chipewyan schools came under fire in terms of failing to maintain academic standards, neglecting to include relevant subject matter about Native history and culture in the curriculum, and "turning out an inferior product in so far as the job market was concerned." Students wishing to complete high school had to relocate to other northern centres such as Fort Smith or Fort McMurray where all twelve grades of schooling were offered. Many who did so soon returned home because they found living away from home too intimidating. Also, since local jobs were scarce, critics felt that schooling did little to prepare students for the reality of the situation. Thus the only realistic expectation of the school was basic literacy, and even then it offered only a substandard form of delivery and limited socialization (Friesen and Boberg, 1990: 151).

A resolution of Fort Chipewyan's schooling dilemma landed in the laps of three parties – government, local educational personnel, and the community. The fact was, however, that the provincial Department of Education was responsible for providing adequate education for all of the province's children. Realistically, this could mean that the same form of education would be provided in every community with some adaptation to local needs.

During the discussion of study results it was pointed out that in northern regions there are many economic implications concerning schooling. For example, people who complete their schooling must also find work, preferably in their home communities. The educational challenge in settlements like Fort Chipewyan therefore concern policy, curriculum, and teaching staff. The stability of the teaching staff has finally been attained, partially aided by an unrelated and somewhat dubious factor, namely the past shortage of jobs for teachers. The move towards local control on the part of Native peoples has also provided a measure of stability and encouraged concern about the relevancy of school curricula in Native communities. School policy, however, must still be modified to reflect local needs.

Things came to a head in Northland after the MacNeil Commission reported and within a few years significant changes were incepted. Among its recommendations the Commission opted for elected school board members rather than their being appointed by the minister as was the tradition. A Northland School Division Investigative Committee was set up to send surveyors to every Northland school community to determine what citizens wanted in terms of schooling in their communities. The committee was to determine what the community's conceptualizations of and preferences for schooling might be. After the investigation was completed an entirely new form of educational administration was initiated. A new Northland School Division Act on June 6, 1983 (Bill 58), gave all eligible residents of each community with an operating school board provision to elect a three to seven person local school board committee. Each of these school boards were then to elect a chairperson who became a member of the Board of Trustees of the Northland School Division and representative of the local area. This board now has the same powers and responsibilities of every other school board in Alberta. At the time of inception the Northland School Division operated 26 schools, hired 193 teachers, and enrolled some 2 500 students.

Camperville, Manitoba

The establishment of workable schools in northern areas has occasionally encountered another obstacle in the form of prejudice, discrimination, and unfair treatment, particularly in integrated situations. A 1973 case study of Camperville, Manitoba drove this point home (Sealey, 1977). At that time the children of Camperville, a Métis community of 700 residents located 300 kilometres north of Winnipeg and 50 kilometres north of Winnipegosis, were bussed to Winnipegosis to complete their high school. There they were faced with what community residents knew to be a long-standing campaign of racism and inequity. A local elementary school in Camperville also failed to meet the needs of the Métis population since it was typical of urban nonNative schools elsewhere in the province, both in terms of curriculum content and school objectives. As a result, a protest was launched on March 15, 1973 when parents of the Métis children conducted a sit-in at the local school. They presented a list of 22 grievances to the school principal and demanded their resolution. The major concerns were alleged prejudice on the part of nonNative teachers towards Métis students, cultural discrimination in regards to forms of dress, racial taunts and insults from Winnipegosis nonNative students and a lack of relevance in the school curriculum which completely omitted any reference to Métis history and culture (Sealey, 1977: 152).

After fruitless local exchanges regarding the format for negotiations, the Manitoba Minister of Education was contacted and he sent two officials to investigate the incident. Student grievances were then referred to the Provincial Human Rights Commission whose targeted investigation focussed on nine alleged infractions of Métis rights. The first pertained to bussing problems to the collegiate, because Métis students were transported home immediately at the end of the school day and thus, unlike resident Winnipegosis students, could not make use of school facilities after school hours. The Human Rights Commission also found incidents of racism on the part of nonNative students, teachers, and townspeople, particularly towards young Métis girls who were often the object of racist taunts and obscenities by some men in the community. The "melting-pot" orientation of both schools was targeted, and it was noted that while these institutions were oriented to a nonNative middle-class lifestyle, the curriculum made absolutely no mention of Métis history and culture. As a result of these and other conditions in all the years that Camperville children had attended high school in Winnipegosis only six students had completed Grade 12 and even then some of them did not pass all Grade 12 departmental exams.

The Human Rights Commission investigated the alleged improprieties and after appropriate investigation issued a report with an attached six-point summary. These included an acknowledgment that Métis students were not being served by the educational program in place at that time. Indeed the dropout rate for Métis high school students was 96 percent, most of them occurring in Grade nine. This was happening during a time when most nonNative Winnipegosis students were graduating from high school. In addition, Métis students entering the local collegiate were one full grade behind their nonNative counterparts on the Canadian Test of Basic Skills. The Commission found evidence of prejudice and discrimination toward the Métis, and concluded that the nonNative middle-class orientation of both schools, elementary and collegiate, ignored Native history. This despite the fact that the elementary school student population in Camperville was 95 percent Métis and the Winnipegosis collegiate had a 28 percent Métis population. No effort was made on the part of school staff to recognize the sociocultural needs of the Métis students, for example, the fact that in the average Camperville home there was no adequate place for students to study because of the very cramped quarters. In general, the atmosphere of the collegiate was to "look down upon Métis students" and the school did not clearly reflect a policy of social integration. Part of the solution posed by the Human Rights Commission was to seek the cooperation of the Camperville and other nearby Métis communities in building a local high school in Camperville. Another concern was to help the local school district in developing a cross-cultural component in the school curriculum that would take cognizance of Native history and culture (Sealey, 1977: 156-157).

The end results of the Camperville investigation were disappointing to say the least. Some changes were effected in the areas specified and a principal who had some knowledge of Aboriginal ways was hired to administrate the Camperville Elementary School. In addition, some cross-cultural training for local teaching staff was made available. A special counsellor at the collegiate was instructed to spend additional time with Métis students and a more positive attitude towards Métis students in the school environment gradually became apparent. The local high school in Camperville never did materialize and Métis students continued to attend high school in Winnipegosis. A decade later, with little or no change in conditions, on April 16, 1984, 350 Métis in Camperville declared themselves an independent nation. They designed and flew a flag declaring absolute jurisdiction over their landspace covering some 500 square kilometres. A primary reason for this move was to attract attention to the Métis desire for self-government. The provincial government ignored the event and within a few days so did the media (Purich, 1988: 158). The situation represents only one of many futile attempts by Native people to try to draw national attention to very unfortunate circumstances.

Analysis

Those students of Métis educational history who look for solutions may be challenged by a Saskatchewan study conducted by Howard Adams which concluded that, all other things being equal, Métis students benefit less from public education than their nonNative counterparts because of: (i) low aspirations; (ii) an inadequate concept of education; and, (iii) social discrimination (Adams, 1972: 30-31). Bruce Sealey discovered two additional factors: (iv) an inadequate self-concept; and, (v) a lack of academic tradition in the family (Sealey, 1977: 162). Add to this a lavish dose of parental apathy brought about by unemployment and disillusionment with their own poor academic records; then combine this with poor student work habits, and educational failure is almost guaranteed (Sealey and Lussier, 1978, Vol. II: 151-152).

Métis educators, Sealey and Lussier, have analyzed the attitudes of teachers working in Native communities with the conclusion that many educators often function according to a series of faulty assumptions. *First,* educators often assume that their students will be unable to function in dominant society without attaining the educational skills which the regular system offers. This is true only if such students involve themselves in life situations where the skills that are taught in provincial schools are required. Students returning to their home communities will not likely find that their educational accomplishments will be of much relevance or applicability.

Second, teachers sometimes employ the term "outside world" when they speak of educational philosophy, as though such a concept is nonexistent in a Native setting. For these educators education in a large urban arena to which it is usually geared, falls into a neat perspective and ties in with the economic base of urban centres. As a result these teachers are unable to think, react, or effectively function within parameters which differ in what they perceive as basic fundamentals (Sealey and Lussier, 1978, Vol. II: 144-245). The result is often frustration, professional dissatisfaction or relocation.

The concept of preparing Native teachers for Native classrooms has been given lip service in western Canadian universities for at least two decades (Friesen, 1985: 42). Following the example of other pioneer institutions, like the University of Saskatchewan and Brandon University, the University of Calgary initiated its Native Outreach Program in 1972. The concept was to provide the first two or three years of teacher education on site in Native communities, and have students complete their degree programs on campus. Early experiments revealed severe difficulties for program participants, particularly with regard to the final year(s) when students were required to relocate to the urban university campus. Often unequipped for big city life with all of its vicissitudes, and often lonely, some returned home instead of finishing their programs of study (Friesen, 1991a). For some years the University of Regina, in conjunction with the Gabriel Dumont Institute of Native Studies and Applied Research sponsored the Saskatchewan Urban Native Teacher Education Program and discovered that urban adjustment on the part of incoming rural-based Indian and Métis students was often a tough challenge. As a result educators devised a support group concept which incorporated a variety of campus structures and events to help such students keep in touch with one another and so bolster their motivation for remaining in the program. This process began with first enrollment and continued after graduation while working in the field. Graduates were also invited back to help with the orientation of first-year students where they stressed the importance of Indian/Métis identity and the importance of the "group" to personal success (Lang and Scarfe, 1985).

As the movement toward local control flourishes in First Nations and Métis communities we will undoubtedly witness significant parallel changes in schooling. Such a move would be indicative of the general Métis "return to roots" movement that has been underground for so long it is only now becoming visible to the nonNative world. In the meanwhile, the Manitoba Métis Federation has staked a land claim to the Red River forks in Winnipeg as well as to the downtown core of the city which they believe they were cheated out of 120 years ago. They also insist that Louis Riel be honored as a Father of Confederation. If this is a visible sign of the rising crescendo of Métis identity, the provision of fair and effective schooling can only fuel the fires of Métis nationalism. Indeed the reality is coming to be, as stated prophetically by Augustine Abraham, a descendant of Louis Riel, ". . . [today] it is fashionable to be Métis" (Robertson, 1992: 102).

Eight

The Twenty-First Century Frontier

Man is born to trouble, as surely as birds fly upwards (Job 5:7). Oh that I had the wings of a dove to fly away and be at rest. (Psalm 55:6 New English Bible)

If they would take some of our advice, they might find a contentment which they are not discovering right now in their mad rush for money and the pleasures which they think it will buy. My Indians can still teach others about living in harmony with nature, and nature still means God or great Spirit or Manitou, depending on what you want to call him. – Stoney Chief Walking Buffalo Tatanga Mani. (MacEwan, 1969: 202)

Wise prophets of every age have been well aware that conflict, disagreement, and unfriendly confrontation are too often the forte of human interaction. When examining the arena of Indigenous rights it is evident that this malaise has not changed much since ancient times. Still, the inclination to "get away from it all" can be supplanted by the realization that nature must be befriended, not destroyed.

As the twenty-first century gets underway, a number of looming frontiers appear to make social and economic progress difficult for Canada's First Nations. These frontiers include land claims, residential school litigations, urban transitions, threats of revisions to the Indian Act, and the possible attainment of some form of Aboriginal self-government. Despite this maze of challenges, it is encouraging to note that progress is being made on some fronts. Some Indian bands, for example, are successfully negotiating with government and private investment companies for the satisfactory development of their natural resources. Others are gaining ground in terms of land and resource settlements. Not surprisingly, the most significant headway is being experienced in educational development. Local control of schooling is now standard fare for many Indian bands, and Native youth are staying in school for longer periods of time and experiencing greater academic achievements.

Statistics pertaining to band-operated schools indicate the proportion of Aboriginal students enrolled in those schools increased from 36 percent in

1988/89 to 58.5 percent in 1997/98. Meanwhile the proportion of Aboriginal students enrolled in federal schools dropped to 1.5 percent in 1998/99 from 16.1 percent in 1988/89. Students also remained in school for longer periods of time. The proportion of Indigenous children who remained in school until grade 12 increased from 39 percent in 1988/89 to a 1997/98 rate of 75 percent (Burns, 2001: 66).

Continuing Frontiers

Aboriginal Self-Government

Some observers view the attainment of Aboriginal self-government as the pivotal point for Indigenous success in other areas. That viewpoint may be challenged, however, if it is perceived as many Native leaders do, that education is the key to a successful future for Canada's Indian people. When the Penner Report was released in 1983 it called for the induction of some form of Aboriginal self-government and introduced the concept of third order government following federal and provincial jurisdictions. Since then the struggle to define self-government has been a continual quest. Essentially, Canada's Indigenous people have been seeking independence and self-determination within Canada for many years, but a workable application of that concept has not been realized. Any attempt at implementing some form of the concept has been fraught with a myriad of doubts and concerns. As Fleras (2000: 121) notes,

> Some see Aboriginal self-government as a "recipe" for social disaster and disunity, others query the soundness of a system based on race and separate status, and still others are worried about the implementation, costs, and jurisdiction. The principle of Aboriginal self-government is criticized as a simplistic solution to a complex problem espoused primarily by Aboriginal elites who are out of touch with urban realities and needs.

The third order of government referred to in the Penner Report has some Aboriginal leaders worried that if some form of it were initiated, it would reduce First Nations' governments to that of glorified municipal governments with very limited powers. In the meantime, the quest for definition has left plenty of fodder for political discussion, Aboriginal worry, and academic rumination.

An outspoken critic of Aboriginal self-government, Flanagan (2000) cautions that the Aboriginal concept of self-determination contributes to cultural exclusiveness. It encourages First Nations to withdrawn unto themselves, under their own "self-governments," on their own "traditional lands," and with their own "Aboriginal economies." Flanagan believes that following down this road will only enable the political and professional elites to do well for themselves at the expense of the good of the majority (Flanagan, 2000: 195). Flanagan is in consensus with Adams (1999) that the contemporary status of neocolonialism in Indian communities encourages upper echelon Natives to adopt conservative middle class ideologies and superimpose them on their unsuspecting peers.

As is well known, the wheels of government grind slowly, partially because representative governance takes time. Parliament committees have to be established followed by the setting of schedules, time-lines, and reports. When this process has satisfactorily come to an end, the controlling political party (if it is still in power), has the choice to enact relevant legislation. On the positive side, governments are consulting more with Indigenous peoples these days, and this democratic requirement can also slow down the wheels of justice.

Land Claims

There are two major categories of land claims now being pursued by the Indigenous peoples in Canada today, comprehensive (Aboriginal title claims), and specific claims. Comprehensive claims largely exist in the north and focus on the demand for formal recognition of Aboriginal land title and rights derived therefrom. Specific claims place more emphasis on cooperation between First Nations and government for the extinguishment of Aboriginal title and restitution of specific rights such as hunting and fishing. Almost all of the Canadian north is being claimed by Indigenous groups, particularly areas in the Arctic, Northwest Territories, and the Yukon. Many land claims are being settled on the basis that First Nations give up their right to the land in exchange for restricted lands, money, certain rights, and benefits for their cultural, social and economic well-being.

Specific land claims are concentrated in British Columbia and Quebec because much land in those two provinces, previously occupied by Indigenous peoples, was never ceded by treaty. More headway in land claims settlements have been made in the prairies and the Maritime provinces, probably because they have affected smaller areas of land.

Residential School Litigations

As previously indicated, there are thousands of cases before Canadian courts pertaining to restitution for sufferings endured by individuals who attended religious residential schools in Canada. The saga continues. As each of the more than 6 000 cases comes before the courts, many are appealed. Those who do achieve restitution frequently receive little compensation, however, because court costs and legal fees absorb most of the monies they are awarded. It remains to be seen if First Nations will be successful in their claims regarding linguistic and cultural losses while being educated in Canadian residential schools.

Urban Transitions

The implementation of any form of Aboriginal self-government will undoubtedly be complicated by the fact that one-third of Canada's Status Indians live off-reserve, most of them in urban areas. A unique development in this area has been the formation of urban reserves. Many Canadian Indians want to be more fully involved in dominant society, not necessarily as assimilated Indians, but as people with a separate cultural integrity. Theoretically, the principle of inherency is based on the notion that self-government is practiced by a national community living on a land base and exercising all the primary social functions typical of any national community. Translating this definition to reality allows the formation of an urban reserve that functions as an extension of a band's national land patrimony and authority. Urban reserves then, were created on the basis of Indian rights contained in the treaties with reference to treaty land entitlements. In Saskatchewan, for example, almost thirty bands were short-changed when land entitlements for reserves were negotiated. As a result, the provincial government has tended to settle with Indian bands by offering them compensatory funds with which to buy private real estate holdings. Some Aboriginal groups who moved to cities, decided to purchase land for the purpose of corporately pursuing economic opportunities. Others saw the creation of urban reserves as an expression of the inherent right of self-government for First Nations (Barron and Garcea, 1999).

Many off-reserve Aboriginals have essentially integrated with dominant society. The question as to how the introduction of Indigenous self-government would affect them is probably only remotely relevant, as is the fact that most of them will likely choose to remain off-reserve. Critics ask, "What then is the point of pumping additional monies into reserve economies when the trend is to move away from them?" As is currently the case, most reserve economies do not support the people who live in there. Most reserve income for Canada's 621 Indian bands is generated off-reserve by nonNatives. Is there any validity to the definition of self-government if it simply means that people living on a reserve have the privilege of spending money generated by someone else (Miller, 2000: 347)?

Boldt (1993: 261) suggests that if Indian cultures are to have any validity in their own right, they must first develop a clear vision and consensus about who they want to be, culturally, in the future. They must assess the damage that colonialists have inflicted on them in the past and invent ways to stop the processes of assimilation and acculturation. They must critically evaluate what must be done to mobilize their people in an effort to make that identity a reality. In Boldt's words,

> Such a process of cultural revitalization will necessitate a purge of corrupting colonial institutions, and of traits derived from the culture of dependence and from Euro-Western acculturation. (Boldt, 1993: 219)

Few observers of the self-government phenomenon are optimistic about fast results. McDonnell and Depew (1999: 353) suggest that "The processes associated with self-government are so powerfully unilateral in their focus that they have all but displaced considerations relating to self-determination." Henderson (2000: 167) accuses legal bureaucrats of unreflectively asserting colonial privileges and power when dealing with the issue, but some observers are a bit more optimistic. Hylton (1999: 432) notes that some progress towards Aboriginal self-government has been made both in terms of federal attitude and experiences reported by some Indian bands. He notes that a number of First Nations have already negotiated far-reaching self-government agreements, and the current federal government appears more willing and better prepared than previous administrations to enter into new arrangements with Aboriginal people.

Indian Act Revisions

The Indian Act was first passed by parliament in 1876 and somewhat modified in later enactments. On May 14, 2001, Robert Nault, Minister of Indian Affairs and Northern Development, proposed changes to the Indian Act to bring it up to date. A discussion paper originated from Nault's office identifying three major concerns: (i) legal standing and capacity of Indian bands and band councils; (ii) leadership selection and voting rights; and, (iii) accountability to First Nations members. Determined to obtain Aboriginal grassroots participation in the amending process, Nault wrote:

> There has been much talk about the First Nations governance initiative. There are rumors about what is being proposed and I want to set the record straight. Firstly, this initiative is not intended to replace treaties or treaty negotiations. And it will not implement self-government. What it will do is provide First Nations operating under the Indian Act with the tools they need to foster responsive and accountable governance. (*Aboriginal Times,* 2001: 34)

In an attempt to obtain feedback to these proposals, Nault's office mailed questionnaires to all First Nations communities in Canada. A *first* concern pointed out by Nault is that under the Indian Act, the powers of chief and council are not clear. The Indian Act does not set out the legal standing and capacity for Indian bands and band councils including such areas as the capacity to sue, to contract, or borrow, all of which make it difficult for band councils to conduct the day-to-day business of their bands.

A *second* concern has to do with leadership selection and voting rights. Currently there are two systems in place – those bands that follow the procedure outlined in the Indian Act via the election of chiefs and councils, and those which follow an hereditary system of appointment. The government has no power to interfere in the latter procedures under the Indian Act. Although the Indian Act now allows off-reserve Aboriginals to vote in band elections, they cannot run for the office of councillor. This does not apply to the office of chief. In fact, one does not have to live on a reserve nor even be a band member to run for that office. It is Nault's impression that many First Nations people want these requirements to change.

The *third* item of concern has to do with accountability. The Indian Act says almost nothing about rules needed to see that First Nations communities are administered on a fair and equitable manner. Many First Nations bands already operate their own systems of accountability, but they vary in form and nature. As it is, Aboriginal band members have virtually no say in such matters as band management of funds or incurred debt load, and the government wants to change this (*Communities First: First Nations Governance Under the Indian Act,* 2001).

Opposition to the government's intention to changing the Indian Act has been strong, particularly from nationally-recognized Indian leaders. Matthew Coon Come, Grand Chief of the Assembly of First Nations (AFN), stated that his organization does not oppose replacing Indian Act, but they want the government to abandon their attempts to reach the grassroots community, and instead work with the Assembly of First Nations (AFN) which represents about half of Canada's Aboriginal people. AFN leaders want the talks to concentrate on Aboriginal self-government, treaty rights and social and economic concerns. Coon Come has threatened to launch campaigns to barricade highways and engage in other disruptions if the government will not desist.

Future Directions for Aboriginal Schooling

As our industrial society continues to thrust changes upon First Nations' communities, Indigenous complaints that they have been hard done by are beginning to be heard. When Native leaders make claims about their youth having been poorly trained in inadequately-equipped schools, managed by unsympathetic administrators, and taught by insensitive teachers, the public appears ready to listen. A few critics may formulate objections such as; "Everyone has had it tough. If you cannot cope with the exigencies of the modern technological age, you will simply have to join the group – get in with the flow. Out-dated traditional practices have no relevance in a competitive society." A harsher tack might be; "Call it assimilation, call it integration, call it adaptation, call it whatever you want; it has to happen" (Flanagan, 2000: 196).

The genius of the Aboriginal perspective is clearly evident in some encouraging adaptations of traditional ways in Canadian schools. In five Niagara Region schools in Ontario, for example, teachers have developed Native support circles in urban schools designed to assist Aboriginal students who have difficulty making the cultural transition from their home communities to that of the urban high school (Pineault and Patterson, 1997). Support circle sessions emphasize Native cultural values and procedures and allow students to talk out personal concerns or raise questions about problematic school programs. Teachers in the Lakehead School Division in Ontario have experimented with a grade nine Aboriginal transition program designed to meet the needs of students who have not achieved intended outcomes in grade eight. The transition program helps students from small and remote communities to ease into an school urban setting. The program is coordinated by a teacher of Native background who delivers an all morning, all year, integrated program to the students in a home-room setting (Palko, Smyth and Stresman, 1993).

Aboriginal students often experience difficulties in adjusting to urban schools because the teachers and students they encounter in urban schools know so little about Native history and cultural traditions. First Nations' cultures emphasize spirituality as a primary focus of learning, while Canadian school curricula rarely include any allusions to either religion or spirituality (McGaa, 1990; Friesen, 2000). Even courses in anti-racist education rarely include enough cultural content about the various ethnocultural communities in Canada to be of much use. Zaraté (1994) makes the point that if it is to be successful the content of anti-racist education must incorporate sufficient cultural knowledge to at least acquaint students with the rudiments of cultural configurations in their home communities. Native students often encounter a wall of ignorance concerning their background when they enroll in urban schools.

Mainstream Canadian schools are not designed to accommodate Aboriginal approaches to teaching/learning. The ancient pedagogical ways of the First Peoples were grounded in extended family relationships. Smith (1997) has formulated six intervention elements for educational policy reform in this regard. He suggests that educators working with First Nations' communities need to: (i) support parents' rights to have a say and participate in the education of their children; (ii) encourage students to maintain their distinct identity, culture, and language; (iii) have access to trained Aboriginal teachers (including elders), to help them maintain cultural and language traditions; (iv) be ready to mediate socio-economic and home difficulties; (v) design classrooms and schools to accommodate extended family structures; and, (vi) try to base all of their plans, actions, and vision on Indigenous values.

Those who have sufficient interest in studying Aboriginal ways will be rewarded in many ways. They will learn about Canada's history before European contact, and personally become enriched through acquaintance with the unique philosophy and lifestyle of Canada's First Peoples. As a result of this study they may discover that Native children approach the teaching/learning milieu differently. In contrast to their nonNative peers, they are taught to be skilful interpreters of silent language, for example – the subtle unspoken communication of facial expressions, gestures, and body movements. In a related study of Indigenous students in Australia, Kaplan and Eckermann (1996) found that Aboriginal student behavior could sometimes be characterized by more boisterous physical activity accompanied by teasing and mild physical aggression between same sex peers and relatives. Indigenous students were found to be more inclined towards touching, sharing, and cuddling than their nonNative counterparts. Native students expected their teachers to touch them and hug them. They were taught that they did not necessarily have to listen to adult instruction unless they wanted to. It was considered culturally acceptable that if students found an activity stressful or boring, they could simply walk away from it. Awareness of the various nuances of Aboriginal perspectives, such as these, will hopefully keep teachers searching for ways to make their approach more meaningful to Native students.

The Final Charge

It has often been said that today's Aboriginal children should be educated to be able to function effectively in both cultural environments, Native and nonNative. While this objective sounds commendable, the question must be raised, "Does that mean they will have to become equally familiar with two distinctly different thought patterns?" Hookimaw-Witt (1998) argues that this is not the case and belittles the notion that education based primarily on Indigenous thinking is not sufficient for survival in the so-called modern world. She contends that EuroCanadian cultural values can be understood and appreciated strictly within the confines of Indigenous perspectives. Any other approach suggests that Indigenous thinking is obsolete or inferior to nonNative approaches. According to Hookimaw-Witt, Aboriginal identity and competence as an Aboriginal person can be reached only when the curriculum is based on the culture from which students draw their identity. If Hookimaw-Witt is right, our schools have a long way to go in understanding and providing for the realization of these objectives.

How can EuroCanadian culture be understood from within the parameters of Aboriginal thought patterns? Only Indigenous people can provide an answer to that question. Presumably they alone have knowledge of how this can come about. Perhaps they have a vision of what will happen to both cultures, Native and NonNative, when this understanding has finally been reached. Now it will be up to them to explain and influence schools systems towards ways of attaining this goal. Because this is so, the final objective of this discussion must necessarily challenge those who alone can make genuine integrated education a reality, that is, Aboriginal people themselves. For this to happen it will require a strong commitment to the worthiness of the campaign. It will also require a unified effort. Only when the various constituents of Indigenous people in Canada come together for the purpose of acquainting nonNative Canadians with their philosophy will the campaign take on any semblance of meaning. Valuing the ancient ways is probably a unanimous stance in Canada's panAboriginal community. How to strengthen and perpetuate it may be subject to a myriad of approaches. There is a need for consensus in developing a workable approach. Isherwood (1997: 24) relates a relevant Mi'kmaq legend about the difficulty of attaining unity and support within the Indigenous community. It is summarized as follows.

> A Mi'kmaq and a nonNative friend went wading in some shallow water to catch some crabs using a net and basket. The crabs were fast swimmers and the men used a dip net to catch them. When a crab was spied the men lowered their dip nets and, with luck, scooped up a crab and dropped it in their basket. The nonNative friend had a lid on his basket, and after each crab was caught and dropped into the basket, he fastened

the lid down so the crab could not escape. The Mi'kmaq had no lid on his basket, but his crabs did not seem to try to escape. The nonNative friend asked the Mi'kmaq why he did not need a lid on his basket. The Mi'kmaq's answer was quick. "I'm catching Mi'kmaq crabs; you're catching nonNative crabs. You see, if a Mi'kmaq tries to get uppity, all the other Mi'kmaq quickly pull him down."

Perhaps one way to avoid the unproductive approach implied in the legend is to replace internal bickering with a more global perspective. Only a unified front will provide the strength that is necessary to attain the respectability of status that Indigenous cultures deserve. Perhaps that day will come. St. Denis (2000) argues that if efforts to make stronger connections between the various forms of resistance are not pursued, then it is likely that Aboriginal people and those from third world countries will continue to see their cultures, resources, and lands exploited. Perhaps Cree lawyer, William Wuttunee is right when he prophesies that "The day will come when Indians will not be concerned with struggling for their basic rights only, but for the basic rights of all individuals" (Friesen, 1998: 65).

Verna Kirkness (1998b: 12-13), a Cree Professor Emeritus at the University of British Columbia, adds another dimension to this conclusion when she urges her own people to meet the challenge of changing times by starting to "cut the mustard." She states:

> To illustrate a point, I would like to suggest that we consider a 4th "R", namely, rhetoric. It is common to hear our political leaders and educators speak eloquently about the importance of education and what we must do to improve it not only for today, but for future generations. We all know the right words; we sound like experts, but we fall short when it comes to putting our rhetoric into action. . . . We say that culture is language and language is culture . . . yet we continue to teach our language for only a few minutes a day in our schools, knowing that this approach is ineffective.

Beatrice Medicine, a respected Lakota anthropologist has a similar view regarding consultation with elders. She charges that the phrase, "My elders tell me," is often used as a meaningless metaphor. Rarely do individuals really consult with elders about issues in the traditional sense. Medicine points out that "Elders are often taken off the shelf just to open a conference with a prayer" (Medicine, 1995: 43). The same attitude applies to the oral tradition which a lot of people talk about but in reality function in a world of literature. Medicine identifies a disparity between the way elders are viewed and the role they actually play in the Native community. The fact is that in some communities elders are abused by their families and constituents and there is little respect for their traditional status and role.

Medicine's observations are well-founded, and she is not alone in making these observations. Cooke-Dallin, Rosborough, and Underwood (2000) note that many elders are complaining that "children don't listen to their Elders anymore." The effect of elder neglect and misuse has had repercussions among elders themselves. Having perceived their role as primarily being one of "conference starter," many elders are now beginning to charge fees for attending public functions. They will not appear at an event unless they are paid. This practice has essentially created a distinction between traditional elders who sincerely and faithfully serve their people, and "circus elders" (not our term), who will make appearances at most any event for the right price. Sadly, most nonNatives are insufficiently acquainted with the nuances of the elder phenomenon to be able to differentiate between the two roles. The good news is that the traditional role of elder is being strengthened in many Aboriginal communities and, hopefully, their testimony will prevail.

The resources to develop healthy First Nations rest in the hands of both Natives and nonNatives. If Kirkness and Medicine are correct, however, the responsibility for a campaign of integration must gain its impetus within the Aboriginal community. Indigenous people alone have in hand the knowledge that is so sorely needed to help Canadians retract their complete disregard for the welfare of the universe. Native people must examine their own hearts and be willing to put their own house in order first, even if it means more pain. NonNatives must not only listen to Aboriginals but they must be willing to implement some of the solutions the latter may consider advisable. Together, we can build a better world for both cultures, Aboriginal and nonAboriginal, in the twenty-first century.

References

Adams, Howard. (1999). *Tortured People: The Politics of Colonization.* Revised edition. Penticton, BC: Theytus Books.

Adams, Howard. 1975). *Prison of Grass: Canada from the Native point of View.* Toronto, ON: New Press.

Adams, Howard. (1972). The Outsiders. Saskatoon, SK: Unpublished paper. Métis Society of Saskatchewan.

Akan, Linda. (1992). Pimosatamowin Sikaw Kakeequaywin: Walking and Talking A Saulteaux Elder's View of Native Education. *Canadian Journal of Native Education,* 19:2, 191-214.

Allison, Derek. (1983). Fourth World Education in Canada and the Faltering Promise of Native Teacher Education. *Journal of Canadian Studies.* 18:3, 102-119.

Anderson, Alan B. and James S. Frideres. (1981). *Ethnicity in Canada: Theoretical Perspectives,* Toronto, ON: Butterworth & Co.

Antone, Eileen M. (2000). Empowering Aboriginal Views in Aboriginal Education. *Canadian Journal of Native Education,* 24:2, 92-101.

Archibald, Jo-ann. (1995). Locally Developed Native Studies Curriculum: An Historical and Philosophical Rationale. *First Nations Education in Canada: The Circle Unfolds.* Marie Battiste and Jean Barman, eds. Vancouver, BC: UBC Press, 288-312.

Ashworth, Mary. (1979). *The Forces Which Shaped Then: A History of Minority Group Children in British Columbia.* Vancouver, BC: New Star Books.

Auger, Ray. (1993). To Learn Another Way: Experiences of Native Students. *Orbit,* 24:1, 14.

Barman, Jean. (1986). Separate and Unequal: Indian and White Girls at All Hallows School, 1884-1920. *Indian Education in Canada, Volume 1: The Legacy.* Jean Barman, Don McCaskill, and Yvonne Hébert, eds. Vancouver, BC: University of British Columbia Press, 110-131.

Barron, F. Laurie and Joseph Garcea. (1999). The Genesis of Urban Reserves and the Role of Governmental Self-Interest. *Urban Indian Reserves: Forging New Relationships in Saskatchewan.* F. Laurie Barron and Joseph Garcea, eds. Saskatoon, SK: Purich Publishing, 22-52.

Bashford, Lucy and Hands Heinzerling. (1987). Blue Quills Native Education Centre: A Case Study. *Indian Education in Canada, Volume 2: The Challenge.* Jean Barman, Don McCaskill, and Yvonne Hébert, eds. Vancouver, BC: University of British Columbia Press, 126-141.

Battiste, Marie. (2000a). Maintaining Aboriginal Identity, Language, and Culture in Modern Society. *Reclaiming Indigenous Voice and Vision.* Marie Battiste, ed. Vancouver, BC: UBC Press, 192-208.

Battiste, Marie, ed. (2000b). *Reclaiming Indigenous Voice and Vision.* Vancouver, BC: UBC Press.

Battiste, Marie and James (Sa'ke'j) Youngblood Henderson. (2000). *Protecting Indigenous Knowledge and Heritage.* Saskatoon, SK: Purich Publishing.

Bear Heart. (1998). *The Wind Is My Mother: The Life and Teachings of a Native American Shaman.* New York: Berkley Books.

Berry, John W. (1981). Native People and the Larger Society. *A Canadian Social Psychology of Ethnic Relations.* Robert C. Gardner and Rudolf Kalin, eds. Toronto, ON: Methuen, 214-230.

Binda, K. P., and Sharilyn Calliou, eds (2001). *Aboriginal Education in Canada: A Study in Decolonization.* Mississauga, ON: Canadian Educators' Press.

Boldt, Menno. (1993). *Surviving as Indians: The Challenge of Self-Government.* Toronto, ON: University of Toronto Press.

Bordewich, Fergus M. (1996). *Killing the White Man's Indian: Reinventing Native Americans at the End of the Twentieth Century.* New York: Anchor Books.

Bowden, Henry Warner. (1981). *American Indians and Christian Missions: Studies in Cultural Conflict.* Chicago, IL: University of Chicago Press.

Brookes, Sonia. (1991). The Persistence of Native Educational Policy in Canada. *The Cultural Maze: Complex Questions on Native Destiny in Western Canada.* John W. Friesen, ed. Calgary, AB: Detselig Enterprises, 163-180.

Brown, Joseph Epes, ed. (1989). *The Sacred Pipe: Black Elk's Account of the Seven Rites of the Oglala Sioux.* Norman, OK: University of Oklahoma Press.

Buckley, Helen. (1993). *From Wooden Ploughs to Welfare: Why Indian Policy Failed in the Prairie Provinces.* Montreal, QC: McGill-Queen's UniversityPress.

Bull, Linda. (1991). Indian Residential Schooling: The Native Perspective. *Canadian Journal of Native Education,* 18: Supplement, 1-63.

Burns, George E. (2001). Finance, Equity, And Equality: Broken Trust In Education. *Aboriginal Education in Canada: A Study in Decolonization.* K. P. Binda and Sharilyn Calliou, eds. Mississauga, ON: Canadian Educators' Press, 59-75.

Burns, George E. (1998). Factors and Themes in Native Education and School Boards/First Nations Tuition Negotiations and Tuition Agreement Schooling. *Canadian Journal of Native Education*, 22:1, 53-66.

Cajete, Gregory. (1994). *Look to the Mountain: An Ecology of Indigenous Education*. Durango, CO: Kivakí Press.

Calliou, Sharilyn. (2001). Situating the Puppet Master. *Aboriginal Education in Canada: A Study in Decolonization*. K. P. Binda and Sharilyn Calliou, eds. Mississauga, ON: Canadian Educators' Press, 1-8.

Calliou, Sharilyn. (1995). Peacekeeping Actions at Home: A Medicine Wheel Model for a Peacekeeping Pedagogy. *First Nations Education in Canada: The Circle Unfolds*. Marie Battiste and Jean Barman, eds. Vancouver, BC: University of British Columbia Press, 47-72.

Calloway, Colin G., ed. (1996). Introduction. *Our Hearts Fell to the Ground: Plains Indian Views of How the West Was Won*. New York: Bedford Books of St. Martin's Press, 1-20.

Campbell, Maria. (1973). *Halfbreed: A Proud and Bitter Canadian Legacy*. Toronto, ON: McClelland and Stewart.

Cardinal, Harold. (1977). *The Rebirth of Canada's Indians*. Edmonton, AB: Hurtig Press.

Cardinal, Harold. (1969). *The Unjust Society: The Tragedy of Canada's Indians*. Edmonton, AB: M. G. Hurtig Ltd.

Chalmers, John W. (1984). Northland: The Founding of a Wilderness School System, *Canadian Journal of Native Education,* 12:2, 2-45.

Chalmers, John W. (1977). Schools for our Other Indians: Education of Western Canadian Métis Children, *The Canadian West,* H. C. Klassen, ed. Calgary, AB: Comprint, 98-108.

Chalmers, John W. (1974). Marguerite Bourgeoys: Preceptress of New France. *Profiles of Canadian Educators*. Robert S. Patterson, John W. Chalmers & John W. Friesen, eds. Toronto, ON: D. C. Heath, 4-20.

Chalmers, John W. (1972). *Education Behind the Buckskin Curtain*. Edmonton, AB: University of Alberta Press.

Chalmers. John W. (1967). *Schools of the Foothills Province: The Story of Public Education in Alberta*. Edmonton, AB: Alberta Teachers' Association.

Churchill, Ward. (1998). A Little Matter of Genocide: Holocaust and Denial in the Americas 1492 to the Present. Winnipeg, MB: Arbeiter Ring Publishing.

Colombo, John Robert. (1987). *Colombo's New Canadian Quotations*. Edmonton, AB: Hurtig Publishers.

Comeau, Larry R. and Leo Driedger (1978). Ethnic Opening and Closing in an Open System: A Canadian Example. *Social Forces,* 57:2, 604-606.

Communities First: First Nations Governance Under the Indian Act. (2001). Ottawa, ON: Published under the authority of the Minister of Indian Affairs and Northern Development.

Communities First: First Nations Governance. (June, 2001). *Aboriginal Times,* 5:8, 34-35.

Cooke-Dallin, Bruce, Trish Rosborough, and Louise Underwood. (2000). The Role of Elders in Child and Youth Care Education. *Canadian Journal of Native Education,* 24:2, 82-91.

Cooper, Michael L. (1999). *Indian School: Teaching the White Man's Way.* New York: Clarion Books.

Copley, John. (January, 2002). Kamloops Church First to Close Over Lawsuits. *Alberta Native News,* 19:1, 31.

Cornish, George H. (1881). *Encyclopedia of Methodism in Canada.* Toronto, ON: Methodist Book and Pub. Co.

Couture, Joseph E. (1991a). Explorations in Native Knowing. *The Cultural Maze: Complex Questions on Native Destiny in Western Canada.* John W. Friesen, ed. Calgary, AB: Detselig Enterprises, 53-76.

Couture, Joseph E. (1991b). The Role of Native Elders. *The Cultural Maze: Complex Questions on Native Destiny in Western Canada.* John W. Friesen, ed. Calgary, AB: Detselig Enterprises, 201-218.

Couture, Joseph E. (1985). Traditional Thinking, Feeling and Learning. *Multicultural Education Journal,* 3:2, 4-16.

Cross, Martin. (December 17, 2001). Aboriginal Leaders Exploiting Their Own Communities. *Mennonite Reporter,* 5:24, 11.

Daniels, E. R. (May, 1967). A.S.T.A. Studies Possible Integration of Indian Students into Provincial Systems. *Alberta School Trustee,* 37:2, 23,

Deloria, Jr., Vine. (1995). *Red Earth, White Lies: Native Americans and the Myth of Scientific Fact.* New York: Scribner.

Dempsey, Hugh A. (1991). The Role of Native Cultures in Western History. *The Cultural Maze: Complex Questions Regarding Native Destiny in Western Canada.* John W. Friesen, ed. Calgary, AB: Detselig Enterprises, 39-52.

Dempsey, Hugh A. (1978). *Indian Tribes of Alberta.* Calgary, AB: Glenbow-Alberta Institute.

Dickason, Olive Patricia. (1993). *Canada's First Nations: A History of Founding Peoples From Earliest Times.* Toronto, ON: McCelland and Stewart.

Dickason, Olive Patricia. (1984). *The Myth of the Savage and the Beginnings of French Colonialism in the Americas.* Edmonton, AB: University of Alberta Press.

Dion, Joseph F. (1996). *My Tribe, The Crees.* Hugh A. Dempsey, ed. Calgary, AB: Glenbow Museum.

Dippie, Brian W. (1985). *The Vanishing American: White Attitudes and the U.S. Indian Policy.* Middletown, CT: Wesleyan University Press.

Dobbin, Murray. (1981). *The One-and-a-Half Men: the Story of Jim Brady and Malcolm Norris, Métis Patriots of the Twentieth Century.* Vancouver, BC: New Star Books.

Driver, Harold E. (1969). *Indians of North America.* Chicago, IL: The University of Chicago Press.

Duff, Wilson. (1997). *The Indian History of British Columbia: The Impact of the White Man.* Victoria, BC: The Royal British Columbia Museum.

Duquette, Cheryll. (2000). Becoming a Teacher: Experiences of First Nations Student Teachers in Isolated Communities. *Canadian Journal of Native Education,* 4:2, 134-143.

Dyck, Noel. (1997). *Differing Visions: Administering Indian Residential Schooling in Prince Albert, 1867-1995.* Halifax, NS: Fernwood Publishing.

Ellis, Clyde. (Summer, 1996). Boarding School Life at the Kiowa-Commanche Agency. *The Historian,* 58:4, 777-784.

Elofson, Warren and Betty-Lou Elofson. (1988). Improving Native Education in the Province of Alberta. *Canadian Journal of Native Education,* 15:1, 31-38.

Ermine, Willie. (1995). Aboriginal Epistemology. *First Nations Education in Canada: The Circle Unfolds.* Marie Battiste and Jean Barman, eds. Vancouver, BC: University of British Columbia Press, 101-112.

Ewers, John C. (1989). *The Blackfeet: Raiders on the Northwestern Plains.* Norman, OK: University of Oklahoma Press.

Farb, Peter. (1968). *Man's Rise to Civilization as Shown by the Indians of North America From Primeval Times to the Coming of the Industrial State.* New York: E. P. Dutton & Co.

Fettes, Mark and Ruth Norton. (2000). Voices of Winter: Aboriginal Languages and Public Policy in Canada. *Aboriginal Education: Fulfilling the Promise.* Marlene Brant Castellano, Lynne Davis and Louise Lahache, eds. Vancouver, BC: UBC Press, 29-54.

Findley, L. M. (2000). *Foreword. Reclaiming Indigenous Voice and Vision.* Marie Battiste, ed. Vancouver, BC: UBC Press, ix-xiii.

Fisher, Robin. (1978). *Contact and Conflict: Indian-European Relations in British Columbia, 1774-1890.* Vancouver, BC: University of British Columbia Press.

Flanagan, Thomas. (2000). *First Nations? Second Thoughts.* Montreal, QC: McGill-Queen's University Press.

Fleras, Augie. (2000). The Politics of Jurisdiction: Pathway or Predicament. *Visions of the Heart: Canadian Aboriginal Issues.* Second edition. David Long and Olive Patricia Dickason, eds. Toronto, ON: Harcourt Canada, 107-142.

Fox, Terry and David Long. (2000). Struggles within the Circle: Violence, Healing and Health on a First Nations Reserve. *Visions of the Heart: Canadian Aboriginal Issues.* Second edition. David Long and Olive Patricia Dickason, eds. Toronto, ON: Harcourt Canada, 271-301.

Frank, Steven. (May 15, 2000). Getting Angry Over Native Rights. *Time,* 155:20, 16-23.

Frideres, James S. (1993). *Native Peoples in Canada: Contemporary Conflicts.* Fourth edition. Scarborough, ON: Prentice-Hall.

Frideres, James S. (1988). *Native Peoples in Canada: Contemporary Conflicts.* Second edition. Scarborough, ON: Prentice-Hall.

Frideres, James S. (1974). *Canada's Indians: Contemporary Conflicts.* Scarborough, ON: Prentice-Hall.

Frideres, James S., and René R. Gadacz. (2001). *Native Peoples in Canada: Contemporary Conflicts.* Sixth edition. Scarborough, ON: Prentice-Hall.

Friedel, Tracy L. (1999). The Role of Aboriginal Parents in Public Education: Barriers to Change in an Urban Setting. *Canadian Journal of Education,* 23:2, 139-158.

Friesen, John W. (2000). *Aboriginal Spirituality and Biblical Theology: Closer Than You Think.* Calgary, AB: Detselig Enterprises.

Friesen, John W. (1999). *First Nations of the Plains: Creative, Adaptable and Enduring.* Calgary, AB: Detselig Enterprises.

Friesen, John W. ed. (1998). *Sayings of the Elders: An Anthology of First Nations' Wisdom.* Calgary, AB: Detselig Enterprises.

Friesen, John W. (1997). *Rediscovering the First Nations of Canada.* Calgary, AB: Detselig Enterprises.

Friesen, John W. (1996). *The Riel/Real Story: An Interpretive History of the Métis People of Canada.* Second edition. Ottawa, ON: Borealis Press.

Friesen, John W. (1995a). *You Can't Get There From Here: The Mystique of North American Plains Indians' Culture & Philosophy.* Dubuque, IA: Kendall/Hunt.

Friesen, John W. (1993a). Formal Schooling Among the Ancient Ones: The Mystique of the Kiva. *American Indian Culture and Research Journal,* 17:4, 55-68.

Friesen, John W. (1995b). *Pick One: A User-Friendly Guide to Religion.* Calgary, AB: Detselig Enterprises.

Friesen, John W. (1993). *When Cultures Clash: Case Studies in Multiculturalism.* second edition. Calgary, AB: Detselig Enterprises.

Friesen, John W. (1991a). Teaching in a University Native Education Program. *The Cultural Maze: Complex Questions on Native Destiny in Western Canada.* John W. Friesen, ed. Calgary, AB: Detselig Enterprises, 229-242.

Friesen, John W. (1991b). Highlights of Western Canadian Indian History. *The Cultural Maze: Complex Questions on Native Destiny in Western Canada.* John W. Friesen, ed. Calgary, AB: Detselig Enterprises, 1-22.

Friesen, John W. (1987a). *Rose of the North.* Ottawa, ON: Borealis Press.

Friesen, John W. (1987b). Language and Cultural Survival: a Myriad of Choices. *Proceedings of the 7th Annual Conference on Native American Language Issues.* Saskatoon, SK: Saskatchewan Indian Language Institute, 83-102

Friesen, John W. (1985). *When Cultures Clash: Case Studies in Multiculturalism.* Calgary, AB: Detselig Enterprises.

Friesen, John W. (1983). *Schools With A Purpose.* Calgary, AB: Detselig Enterprises.

Friesen, John W. (1977). *People, Culture & Learning.* Calgary, AB: Detselig Enterprises.

Friesen, John W. (1974). John McDougall, Educator of Indians. *Profiles of Canadian Educators.* Robert S. Patterson, John W. Chalmers and John W. Friesen, eds. Toronto, ON: D. C. Heath, 57-76.

Friesen, John W. and Alice L. Boberg. (1990). *Introduction to Teaching: A Sociocultural Approach.* Dubuque, IA: Kendall/Hunt.

Friesen, John W. and Michael M. Verigin. (1996). *The Community Doukhobors: A People in Transition.* Second edition. Ottawa, ON: Borealis Press.

Frontier School Division No. 48. (2000). Winnipeg, MB: Province of Manitoba.

Fulham, S. (1972). *In Search of a Future.* Winnipeg, MB: Manitoba Métis Federation Press.

Fumoleau, Rene. (1973). *As Long as This Land Shall Last: A History of Treaty 8 and Treaty 11, 1870-1939.* Toronto, ON: McClelland and Stewart.

Furniss, Elizabeth. (1995). *Victims of Benevolence: The Dark Legacy of the Williams Lake Residential School.* Vancouver, BC: Arsenal Pulp Press.

Giraud, Marcel. (Winter, 1956). The Western Métis After the Insurrection, *Saskatchewan History,* IX:1, 1-15.

Goddard, John. (1992). *Last Stand of the Lubicon Cree.* Vancouver, BC: Douglas and McIntyre.

Goldenweiser, Alexander A. (1968). *Iroquois Social Organization The North American Indians: A Sourcebook.* Roger C. Owen, James J. F. Deetz, and Anthony D. Fisher, eds. New York: Collier-Macmillan, 565-575.

Goulet, Linda (2001). Two Teachers of Aboriginal Students: Effective Practice in Sociohistorical Realities. *Canadian Journal of Native Education,* 25:1, 68-82.

Goulet, Linda, Marjorie Dresseyman-Lavallee, and Yvonne McCleod. (2001). *Aboriginal Education in Canada: A Study in Decolonization.* K. P. Binda and Sharilyn Calliou, eds. Mississauga, ON: Canadian Educators' Press, 137-153.

Grant, Agnes. (1996). *No End of Grief: Indian Residential Schools in Canada.* Winnipeg, MB: Pemmican Publications.

Gresko, Jacqueline. (1986). Creating Little Dominions Within the Dominion: Early Catholic Indian Schools in Saskatchewan and British Columbia. *Indian Education in Canada, Volume 1:* The Legacy. Jean Barman, Don McCaskill, and Yvonne Hébert, eds. Vancouver, BC: University of British Columbia Press, 88-109.

Gresko, Jacqueline. (1979). White 'Rites' and Indian 'Rites': Indian Education and Native Responses In the West, 1870-1910. *Shaping the Schools of the Canadian West.* David C. Jones, Nancy M. Sheehan, and Robert Stamp, eds. Calgary, AB: Detselig Enterprises, 84-108.

Grinnell, George Bird. (1962). *Blackfoot Lodge* Tales. Lincoln, NE: University of Nebraska Press.

Haig-Brown, Celia. (1993). *Resistance and Renewal: Surviving the Indian Residential School.* Vancouver, BC: Tillacum Library.

Hampton, Eber. (2000). First Nations Controlled University Education in Canada. *Aboriginal Education: Fulfilling the Promise.* Marlene Brant Castellano, Lynne Davis and Louise Lahache, eds. Vancouver, BC: UBC Press, 208-223.

Hanohano, Peter. (1999). The Spiritual Imperative of Native Epistemology: Restoring Harmony and Balance to Education. *Canadian Journal of Native Education,* 23:2, 206-219.

Hare, Jan and Jean Barman. (2000). Aboriginal Education: Is There a Way Ahead? *Visions of the Heart: Canadian Aboriginal Issues.* Second edition. David Long and Olive Patricia Dickason, eds. Toronto, ON: Harcourt Canada, 331-360.

Harrod, Howard L. (1992). *Renewing the World: Plains Indians Religion and Morality.* Tucson, AZ: University of Arizona Press.

Hawthorn, H. B., ed. (1966 and 1967). *Survey of Contemporary Indians of Canada.* Two volumes, Ottawa, ON: Indian Affairs Branch.

Healy, Sharron. (1983). Assiniboine Creation Story. *Assiniboine Memories: Legends of the Nakota People.* Fort Belknap, MT: Fort Belknap Education Department, 1-2.

Henderson, James (Sa'ke'j) Youngblood. (2000). Postcolonial Ledger Drawing: Legal Reform. *Protecting Indigenous Knowledge and Heritage.* Marie Battiste and James (Sa'ke'j) Youngblood, eds. Saskatoon, SK: Purich Publishing, 172-178.

Hildebrandt, Walter, Sarah Carter and Dorothy First Rider. (1996). *The True Spirit and Original Intent of Treaty 7: Treaty Elders and Tribal Council.* Montreal, PQ: McGill/Queen's University Press.

Hodgeson-Smith, Kathy L. (2000). Issues of Pedagogy in Aboriginal Education. *Aboriginal Education: Fulfilling the Promise.* Marlene Brant Castellano, Lynne Davis and Louise Lahache, eds. Vancouver, BC: UBC Press,156-175.

Hoebel, E. Adamson. (1965). *The Cheyennes: Indians of the Great Plains.* New York: Holt, Rinehart and Winston.

Hookimaw-Witt, Jacqueline. (1998). Any Changes Since Residential School? *Canadian Journal of Native Education,* 22:2, 159-170.

House, Earnest R. (1992). Multicultural Evaluation in Canada and the United States. *The Canadian Journal of Program Evaluation,* 7:1, 133-156.

Hoxie, Frederick E. (1989). *The Crow.* New York: Chelsea House Publishers.

Hungry Wolf, Adolf, and Beverly Hungry Wolf. (1991). *Indian Tribes of the Northern Rockies.* Skookumchuck, BC: Good Medicine Books.

Hylton, John H. (1999). Future Prospects for Aboriginal Self-Government in Canada. *Aboriginal Self-Government in Canada.* John H. Hylton, ed. Saskatoon, SK: Purich Publishing, 432-455.

Ing, N. Rosalyn. (1991). The Effects of Residential Schools on Native Child-Rearing Practices. *Canadian Journal of Native Education.* 18:Supplement, 65-118.

Isherwood, Geoffrey B. (1997). Developing Native School Boards: Facilitators and Impediments. *Education Canada,* 37:2, 22-27.

Jaenen, Cornelius. (1986). Education for Francization: The Case of New France in the Seventeenth Century. *Indian Education in Canada, Vol.1:* The Legacy. Jean Barman, Don McCaskill, and Yvonne Hébert, eds. Vancouver, BC: University of British Columbia Press, 45-63.

Jennings, D. (1978). *Origins. Ancient Native Americans.* D. Jennings, ed. San Francisco, CA: W. H. Freeman and Company.

Johnson, F. Henry. (1968). *A Brief History of Canadian Education.* Toronto, ON: McGraw-Hill.

Johnston, Basil. (1995). *The Manitous: The Spiritual World of the Ojibway.* Vancouver, BC: Key Porter Books.

Josephy, Jr., Alvin M. (1989). *Now That the Buffalo's Gone: A Study of Today's American Indians.* Norman, OK: University of Oklahoma Press.

Josephy, Jr., Alvin M. (1968). *The Indian Heritage of America.* New York: Alfred A. Knopf.

Jull, Peter. (1992). *Lessons from Indigenous Peoples. Sweet Promises: A Reader on Indian-White Relations in Canada.* J.R. Miller, ed. Toronto, ON: University of Toronto Press, 452-458.

Kaltreider, Kurt. (1998). *American Indian Prophecies: Conversations with Chasing Deer.* Carlsbad, CA: Hay House.

King, A. Richard. (1967). *The School At Mopass: A Problem of Identity.* New York: Holt, Rinehart & Winston.

Kirk, Ruth. (1986). *Wisdom of the Elders: Native Traditions on the Northwest Coast.* Vancouver, BC: Douglas and McIntyre.

Kirkness, Verna J. (1998a). The Critical State of Aboriginal Languages in Canada. *Canadian Journal of Native Education,* 22:1, 93-107.

Kirkness, Verna J. (1998b). Our Peoples' Education: Cut the Shackles; Cut the Crap; Cut the Mustard. *Canadian Journal of Native Education,* 22:1, 10-15.

Kirkness, Verna J. (July/August, 1981). The Education of Canadian Indian Children. *Child Welfare,* LX:7, 446-455.

Kirkness, Verna J., and Sheena Selkirk Bowman. (1983). *First Nations and Schools: Triumphs and Struggles.* Toronto, ON: Canadian Education Association.

Knill, William D. and Arthur K. Davis. (1966). Provincial Education in Northern Saskatchewan: Progress and Bog-Down, 144-162, *A Northern Dilemma: Reference Papers, Vol. 1,* Arthur K. Davis, ed. Bellingham, WA: Western Washington State College, 170-337.

Knockwood, Isabelle, with Gillian Thomas. (1994). *Out of the Depths: The Experience of Mi'kmaw Children at the Indian Residential School at Shubenacadie, Nova Scotia.* Lockeport, NS: Roseway Publishing.

Knudtson, Peter and David Suzuki. (1992). *Wisdom of the Elders.* Toronto, ON: Stoddart.

Lagasse, Jean H., Director. (1959). *A Study of the Population of Indian Ancestry living in Manitoba.* Three Volumes. Winnipeg, MB: Department of Agriculture and Immigration.

Lame Deer, John (Fire) and Richard Erdoes. (1972). *Lame Deer: Seeker of Visions.* New York: Simon and Schuster.

Lang, H. R. and D. R. Scarfe. (1985). *The Group as Support in a Native Teacher Education Program.* Montreal, PQ: The Canadian Association of Teacher Educators, Canadian Society for the Study of Education.

Leavitt, Robert. (1995). Language and Cultural Content in Native Education. *First Nations Education in Canada: The Circle Unfolds.* Marie Battiste and Jean Barman, eds. Vancouver, BC: UBC Press, 124-138.

Ledgerwood, C.D. (1972). *Native Education in the Province of Alberta.* Edmonton, AB: Minister of Education, Government of Alberta.

Lincoln, Kenneth. (1985). *Native American Renaissance.* Berkeley, CA: University of California Press.

Littlebear, Dick. (1992). Getting Teachers and Parents to Work Together. *Teaching American Indian Students,* Jon Reyhner, ed. Norman, OK: University of Oklahoma Press, 104-114.

Long, David and Patricia Dickason, eds. (2000). *Visions of the Heart: Canadian Aboriginal Issues. Second edition.* Toronto, ON: Harcourt Canada.

Looking Horse, Arval. (1988). The Sacred Pipe in Modern Life. *Sioux Indian Religion.* Raymond J. DeMallie and Douglas R. Parks, eds. Norman, OK: University of Oklahomoa Press, 67-74.

Lowie, Robert H. (1963). *Indians of the Plains.* New York: The Natural History Press.

Lowie, Robert H. (1956). *The Crow Indians.* New York: Holt, Rinehart and Winston.

Lupul, Manoly R. (1970). Education in Western Canada Before 1873. *Canadian Education: A History.* J. Donald Wilson, Robert M. Stamp, and Louis-Philippe Audet, eds. Scarborough, ON: Prentice-Hall, 241-264.

Lusty, Terrance. (1973). *Louis Riel: Humanitarian.* Calgary, AB: Northwest Printing Co.

MacEwan, Grant. (1981). *Métis Makers of History.* Saskatoon, SK: Western Producer Books.

MacEwan, Grant. (1969). *Tatanga Mani: Walking Buffalo of the Stonies.* Edmonton, AB: M. G. Hurtig Publishers Ltd.

MacNeil, Harold, Chair. (1981). *Report of the Northland School Division Investigation Committee.* Edmonton, AB: Department of Education.

Marker, Michael. (2000). Economics and Local Self-Determination: Describing the Clash Zone in First Nations Education. *Canadian Journal of Native Education,* 24:1, 30-44.

McDonald, N. G. (1974). David J. Goggin: Promoter of National Schools. *Profiles of Canadian Educators.* Robert S. Patterson, John W. Chalmers and John W. Friesen, eds. Toronto, ON: D. C. Heath, 167-191.

McDonnell, R. F. and R. C. Depew. (1999). Self-Government and Self-Determination in Canada: A Critical Commentary. *Aboriginal Self-Government in Canada.* John H. Hylton, ed. Saskatoon, SK: Purich Publishing, 352-376.

McDougall, John. (1903). *In the Days of the Red River Rebellion.* Toronto, ON: William Briggs.

McGaa, Ed Eagle Man. (1995). *Native Wisdom: Perceptions of the Natural Way.* Minneapolis, MN: Four Directions Publishing.

McGaa, Ed Eagle Man. (1990). *Mother Earth Spirituality: Native American Paths to Healing Ourselves and Our World.* San Francisco, CA: Harper

Medicine, Beatrice. (1995). Prologue to a Vision of Aboriginal Education. *Canadian Journal of Native Education,* 21: Supplement, 42-45.

Medicine, Beatrice. (1987). My Elders Tell Me. *Indian Education in Canada: the Challenge, Volume 1: the Legacy* Jean Barman, Don McCaskill, and Yvonne Hébert, eds. Vancouver, BC: University of British Columbia Press, 142-152.

Meili, Dianne. (1992). *Those Who Know: Profiles of Alberta's Native Elders.* Edmonton, AB: NeWest.

Melling, John. (1967). *Right to a Future: The Native Peoples of Canada.* Don Mills, ON: T.H. Best Printing Company.

Miller, J. R. (2000). *Skyscrapers Hide the Heavens: A History of Indian-White Relations in Canada.* Third edition. Toronto, ON: University of Toronto Press.

Miller, J. R. (1997). *Shingwauk's Vision: A History of Native Residential Schools.* Toronto, ON: University of Toronto Press.

Miller, J. R., ed. (1992). *Sweet Promises: A Reader in Indian-white Relations in Canada.* Toronto, ON: University of Toronto Press.

Miller, J. R. (1987). The Irony of Residential Schooling. *Canadian Journal of Native Education.* 14:2, 3-14.

Milloy, John S. (1999). *A National Crime: The Canadian Government and the Residential School System, 1879 to 1986.* Winnipeg, MB: University of Manitoba Press.

Morgan, Lewis H. (1963). *Ancient Society.* Cleveland, OH: World Publishing.

Morris, Joann Sebastian , and Richard T. Price. (1991). Community Control Issues and the Experience of Alexander's Kipohtakaw Education Centre. *The Cultural Maze: Complex Questions on Native Destiny in Western Canada.* John W. Friesen, ed. Calgary, AB: Detselig Enterprises, 181-198.

Nicholas, Andrea Bear. (2001). Canada's Colonial Mission: The Great White Bird. *Aboriginal Education in Canada: A Study in Decolonization.* K. P. Binda and Sharilyn Calliou, eds. Mississauga, ON: Canadian Educators' Press, 9-33.

Norman, Howard, ed. (1990). *Northern Tales: Traditional Stories of Eskimo and Indian Peoples.* New York: Pantheon Books.

Outerbridge, Ian. (September, 2000). Residential Schools: Finding a Way Through the Debacle. *Fellowship Magazine,* 18:3, 4-7.

Owen, Roger C., James J. F. Deetz, and Anthony D. Fisher, eds. (1968). *The North American Indians: A Sourcebook.* New York: The Macmillan Company.

Palko, John, Elizabeth Smyth and Elsie Stresman. (1993). The Grade 9 original Transition Program. *Orbit,* 24:3, 30-31.

Paupanekis, Kenneth, and David Westfall. (2001). Teaching Native Language Programs: Survival Strategies. *Aboriginal Education in Canada: A Study in Decolonization.* K. P. Binda and Sharilyn Calliou, eds. Mississauga, ON: Canadian Educators' Press, 89-104.

Patterson II, E. Palmer. (1972). *The Canadian Indian: A History Since 1500.* Don Mills, ON: Collier-Macmillan Canada.

Patterson, Robert S., John W. Chalmers, and John W. Friesen, eds. (1974). *Profiles of Canadian Educators.* Toronto, ON: D.C. Heath.

Pauls, Syd. (1984). The Case for Band-controlled Schools. *Canadian Journal of Native Education.* 12:1, 31-37.

Pelletier, Wilfred. (1974). Two articles. Toronto: Neewin Publishing Co., quoted in J. S. Frideres. (1974). *Canada's Indians: Contemporary Conflicts.* Scarborough, ON: Prentice-Hall, 105-106.

Perley, David G. (1993). Aboriginal Education in Canada as Internal Colonialism. *Canada Journal of Native Education*, 20:1, 118-128.

Persson, Diane. (1986). The Changing Experience of Indian Residential Schooling: Blue Quills, 1931-1970. *Indian Education in Canada, Vol. 1: The Legacy.* Jean Barman, Don McCaskill, and Yvonne Hébert, eds. Vancouver, BC: University of British Columbia Press, 150-168.

Pineault, Ann, and Claire Patterson. (1997). Native Support Circles in Urban Schools. *Orbit,* 28:1, 27-29.

Ponting, J. Rick. (1997). Getting a Handle on Recommendations of the Royal Commission on Aboriginal Peoples. *First Nations in Canada: Perspectives on Opportunity, Empowerment, and Self-Determination* J. Rick Ponting, ed. Toronto, ON: McGraw-Hill Ryerson, 445-472.

Porterfield, Amanda. (1990). American Indian Spirituality as a Countercultural Movement. *Religion in Native North America.* Christopher Vecsey, ed. Moscow, ID: University of Idaho Press, 152-166.

Purich, Don. (1988). *The Métis.* Toronto, ON: James Lorimer.

Purich, Don. (1986). *Our Land: Native Rights in Canada.* Toronto, ON: James Lorimer.

Ray, Arthur J. (1974). *Indians in the Fur Trade: Their Role as Trappers, Hunters, and Middlemen in the Lands Southwest of Hudson Bay, 1660-1870.* Toronto, ON: University of Toronto Press.

Reyhner, Jon. (1992). *Teaching American Indian Students.* Norman, OK: University of Oklahoma Press.

Robertson, Heather. (March/April, 1992). Canada Journal: The Forks, Manitoba: Shaking the Spirit of Louis Riel, *Equinox,* 62: 83-102.

Rogers, Edward S. (1994). The Algonquian Farmers of Southern Ontario, 1830-1945. *Aboriginal Ontario: Historical Perspectives on the First Nations.* Edwards S. Rogers and Donald B. Smith, eds. Toronto, ON: Dundurn Press, 122-166.

Ross, Rupert. (1992). *Dancing With A Ghost: Exploring Indian Reality.* Markham, ON: Reed Books.

Savage, Brian. (February, 2002). Order of Oblates Fights Court Decision. *Alberta Native News,* 19:2, 20.

Schneider, Mary Jane. (1989). *The Hidatsa.* New York: Chelsea House Publishers.

Sealey, D. Bruce. (1980). *The Education of Native Peoples in Manitoba.* Monographs in Education, No. III, Winnipeg, MB: University of Manitoba.

Sealey, D. Bruce. (1977). The Métis: Schools, Identity and Conflict. *Canadian schools and Canadian Identity.* Alf Chaiton and Neil McDonald, eds. Toronto, ON: Gage Educational Publishing, 150-164.

Sealey, D. Bruce and Antoine S. Lussier (1978). *The Other Natives: the-les Métis, Vol. I, 1700-1885, Vol. II, 1885-1978.* Winnipeg, MB: Manitoba Métis Federation Press.

Sealey, D. Bruce and Antoine Lussier. (1975). *The Métis: Canada's Forgotten People.* Winnipeg, MB: Manitoba Métis Federation Press.

Sealey, D. Bruce and Verna J. Kirkness. (1973). *Indians Without Tipis: A Resource Book by Indians and Métis.* Vancouver, BC: William Clare.

Shaffer, Lynda Norene. (1992). *Native Americans Before 1492: The Moundbuilding Centers of the Eastern Woodlands.* Armonk, NY: M.E. Sharpe.

Smith, Douglas James. (Spring, 1997). Indigenous Peoples' Extended Family Relationships: A Source for Classroom Structure. *McGill Journal of Education,* 32:2, 125-138.

Snow, Chief John. (1977). *These Mountains Are Our Sacred Places: The Story of the Stoney Indians.* Toronto, ON: Samuel Stevens.

St. Denis, Verna. (Spring, 2000). Indigenous Peoples, Globalization, and Education: Making Connections. *The Alberta Journal of Educational Research,* XLVI:1, 36-48.

Stairs, Arlene. (1995). Learning Processes and Teaching Roles in Native Education: Cultural Base and Cultural Brokerage. *First Nations Education in Canada: The Circle Unfolds.* Marie Battiste and Jean Barman, eds. Vancouver, BC: University of British Columbia Press, 139-153.

Surtees, R. J. (1969). The Development of an Indian Reserve Policy in Canada. *Ontario Historical Society.* LXI, 897-899.

Suzuki, David. (1997). *The Sacred Balance: Rediscovering Our Place in Nature.* Vancouver, BC: Douglas & McIntyre.

Suzuki, David. (1992). A Personal Foreword: The Value of Native Ecologies.*Wisdom of the Elders* by Peter Knudtson and David Suzuki. Toronto, ON: Stoddart, xxi-xxvi.

Taylor, John. (1995). Non-Native Teachers Teaching in Native Communities. *First Nations Education in Canada: The Circle Unfolds.* Marie Battiste and Jean Barman, eds. Vancouver, BC: UBC Press, 224-242.

Titley, E. Brian. (1992). Red Deer Indian Industrial School: A Case Study in the History of Native Education. *Exploring Our Educational Past.* Nick Kach and Kas Mazurek, eds. Calgary, AB: Detselig Enterprises, 55-72.

Tobias, J. L. (1988). Indian Reserves in Western Canada: Indian Homelands or Devices for Assimilation? *Native People: Native Lands.* Bruce Alden Cox, ed. Ottawa, ON: Carleton University Press, 148-157.

Treaty 7 and Tribal Council with Walter Hildebrandt, Dorothy First Rider and Sarah Carter. (1996). *The True Spirit and Original Intent of Treaty 7.* Montreal, QC: McGill-Queen's University Press.

Tremblay, Paulette C. (2001). First Nations Educational Jurisdiction: National Background Paper. Ottawa, ON: Educational Sector, Assembly of First Nations.

Tsuji, Leonard J. S. (2000). Modified School Years: An Important Issue of Local Control. *Canadian Journal of Native Education,* 24:2, 158-168.

Underhill, Ruth M. (1965). *Red Man's Religion: Beliefs and Practices of the Indians North of Mexico.* Chicago, IL: University of Chicago Press.

Weaver, Jace, ed. (1998). *Native American Religious Identity: Unforgotten* Gods. Maryknoll, NY: Orbis Books.

Weber-Pillwax, Cora. (April, 1999). Indigenous Research Methodology: Exploratory Discussion of an Elusive Subject. *The Journal of Educational Thought,* 33:11, 31-46.

Wilson, David. (November, 2000). Residential Schools: History on Trial. *The United Church Observer,* 64:4, 28-31.

Witt, Norbert. (1998). Promoting Self-Esteem, Defining Culture. *Canadian Journal of Native Education,* 22:2, 260-273.

Wolcott, Harry F. (1967). *A Kwakiutl Village and School.* New York: Holt, Rinehart and Winston.

Woodward, Joe. (November 4, 2000). Caribou Bishop Cruickshank Speaks on the Need for Healing, and Being Bankrupt. *Calgary Herald,* 0S10.

Wuttunee, William. (1971). *Ruffled Feathers: Indians in Canadian Society.* Calgary, AB: Bell Books.

Yazzie, Robert. (2000). Indigenous Peoples and Postcolonial Colonialism. *Reclaiming Indigenous Voice and Vision.* Marie Battiste, ed. Vancouver, BC: UBC Press, 39-49.

Zaraté, José. (1994). Indigenous Knowledge and Anti-Racist Education. *Orbit,* 25:2, 35-36.

Index

A Plan to liquidate Canada's Indian
 Problem in twenty-five years 108
Acadia 81
Act for the Gradual Civilization of the
 Indian 82, 103
Adams, Howard 23, 119, 121, 133, 139
Aesop's fables 73
Alberta 25, 124
Alberta Glenbow Museum 161
Anasazi 43
Anglican 102, 105, 115
Arapahos 66
Arctic 139
Arikara 51, 53
Aryan 40
Assembly of First Nations (AFN) 92,
 93, 94, 100, 142
Assiniboines 65
Atomism 37
Australia 144

Beaver First Nation 66
Bering Strait theory 42, 43
Blackfeet Nation 17, 58
Blackfoot, Blackfoot Nation 19, 58, 63,
 66
Blood Tribe 17, 48
Blue Quills, AB 14, 92, 93
Bourgeoys, Sister Marquerite 83, 101
Brady, Jim 122
Brandon University 134
British Columbia 43, 85, 87, 105, 115,
 139
British Empire 84
Brown Paper 91, 92
Buffalo 54
Buffalo calling ceremony 51

Camperville, MB 131, 132, 133
Canadian Métis Society 92
Capauchins 81

Carrier 63
Cartier, Jacques 81
Charter Nations 39
Cheyennes 58, 59, 66
Chippewa 84
Chrétien, the Honourable Jean 90, 95
Christmas 33
Citizen's plus 90
Civil rights 90
Civilization and Enfranchisement Act 82
Clan 52, 60
Clovis People 42
Coal Bear 59
Collier, John 41
Colonization 22
Come Coon, Matthew 100, 142, 143
Confederation 87
Couture, Joseph 55, 63
Coyote 66, 69
Cree(s) 54, 55, 84, 124
Crow Indians 52
Cultural genocide 15
Cultural renaissance 16, 60
Curricula, curriculum 31, 33, 34, 35, 93

Davin, Nicholas Flood 105, 106, 121
Davin Report 87
de Champlain, Samuel 81
Deloria Jr., Vine 42, 43
Demers, Modeste 85
Dene 124
Department of Aboriginal Relations 95
Department of Canadian Heritage 79
Department of Indian and Inuit Services
 95
Devil's Tower 58
Dickason, Olive 39
Dion, Joe 54
Dogrib 72
Duncan, William 85

Earth reverence 49
Eastern Woodlands 43
Elder(s) 35, 44, 47, 63, 68, 69, 73, 74, 78, 79, 147
Erasmus, Chief George 95
Evans, James 85, 86

Family 50, 52, 53, 60
First occupancy 76
Flanagan, Thomas 23, 96, 138, 139
Fontaine, Phil 95, 100, 117
Fort Chipewyan, AB 55, 130
Four Guns 47
Franciscans 81
Frontier School Division 127
Fur traders 77

Gabriel Dumont Institute 134
Give-away dance 54
Glen, J. Allison 88
Global, global warming 41, 45
Glooscap 72
Goggin, David 86, 87, 122
Great Lake Region 43
Great Mystery 41
Grey Nuns 85, 102
Grimm's fairy tales 73

Haida 85
Harper, Elijah 95
Hawthorn, Harry 90
Hawthorn Report 26
Hidatsa 51, 53
High context cultures 27
Hohokam 43
Holistic 61
House of First Peoples 95
Hudson's Bay Company 85, 86, 101
Hugonnard, Father Joseph 85, 86
Huron Confederacy 52
Hurons 81
Hutterite 126

Ikûmnî 65, 69
In Search of a Future 128
Indian Act 13, 39, 82, 87, 88, 91, 137, 141, 142

Indian Advancement Act of 1884 82
Indian Status 90
Indian time 51
Indigenous knowledge 35, 36, 37, 44
Individuality 32
Industrial schools 87, 88
Interconnectedness 45, 47
Inuit 56, 80, 96
Iroqouis League 52

Jesuits 83
Jenness, Diamond 88
Jones, Peter 103
Joseph, Chief 57

Kainai Nation 17
Kirkness, Verna 146

La Flesche, Susan 100
Lacombe, Rev. Albert 85, 102
Laing, Arthur 88
Lake Winnipeg 65
Lakota Sioux 41
Lame Deer 58
Land claims 98, 139
Language 29, 30, 39, 60, 61, 79, 96
Laurier Liberal Government 106, 107
Learning styles 31, 32
Legends, legend telling 67, 68, 69, 70, 71, 72, 73, 74, 75
Local control of schooling 137

Macdonald, Prime Minister John A. 106
MacNeil Commission 129, 131
MacPherson, James 94
MacPherson Report 94
Mandan Indians 51, 53
Manitoba 84, 85, 119, 121, 122, 126
Manitoba Métis Federation 119, 135
Manning, Premier Ernest 91
McDougall, George 85, 86
McDougall, John 85, 86
Medicine, Beatrice 146, 147
Medicine bundle 58

Melting-pot 132
Mennonite Native Ministries 23
Methodist 85, 102, 103
Métis 96, 119f
Métis Association of Alberta 121
Micmac 72, 81, 84
Mi'kmaq 98, 145, 146
Mission schools 82
Montana 17
Moose Division 125
Moundbuilders 43
Mulroney, Prime Minister Brian 95
Multicultural 76
Music 112

Nakoda Sioux 71
Name-calling 57
Napi 69
National Indian Brotherhood 92, 93
Native Outreach Program 134
Nault, Robert 141, 142
Navajo 109
New Brunswick 84
New England Company 84
New France 81, 83, 84, 101
New Zealand 88
Nicholas, Andrea Bear 24
Nisga' 98
Non-Status 92, 96, 119, 124
North Dakota 51
Northern Lights School Division 124
Northland School Division 124, 125,
  128, 129

Oblates 102
Ojibway, 103, 105
Ontario 25, 103, 105, 143
Oral tradition 64, 65, 67, 68, 74, 76

Paleo Indians 42
Parker, Charles 121
Pawnees 58
Pedagogy 63, 64, 77
Pedley, Frank 107
Peguis 105

Peigan nation 17
Penner Report 138
Pipe ceremonies 44
Plateau Indians 34, 43
Post-secondary education 80
Potawatomi 58
Potlatch 44
Precontact 44, 53
Presbyterians 115
Prophet Amos 52
Provincial Human Rights Commission
  132

Quebec 139

Red Fox, Chief 45
Red Paper 90, 91
Red power 90
Residential school litigations 115, 137,
  140
Residential schools 87, 92, 95, 99f,
  143
Riel, Louis 119, 135
Riel War 86
Rough Rock, AZ 109
Royal Commission on Aboriginal
  Peoples 95, 96, 97
Royal Proclamation 95
Ruffled Feathers 91
Rundle, Rev. Robert 85
Ryerson, Egerton 87, 103

Sacred Buffalo Hat 58, 59
Sacred Chief Drum 58, 59
Sacred Horns 59
Sacred Medicine Arrows 58, 59
Sarcee Nation 66
Saskatchewan 25, 112, 113, 121, 122,
  140
Scott, Duncan Campbell 107
Sealey, Bruce 133
Self-government 94, 98, 137, 138
Seven Council Fires 65
Sharing 53, 54
Sifton, Clifford 106, 107

Siksika 17, 19
Sisters of Charity 85
Snow, Chief John ix, 13, 17, 70, 78
South Dakota 42
Spears, Britney 19
Spiritual, spirituality 21, 30, 33, 37,
   39, 44, 45, 57
Staines, Rev. Robert 85
Status Indians 80
Steinhauer, Henry 85
Stoney, Stoney First Nation 13, 72, 73,
   74, 78, 86
Storytelling 47, 53
St. Luke 21
St. Paul, AB 109
Suzuki, David 18, 41, 45, 74
Sweet Medicine 58
Sweetgrass 44, 64

Teacher education 28, 29
Teachers 27, 28, 32, 35, 80, 93, 122,
   134
Tecumseh, Chief 50
Thorpe, Jim 100
Tobacco 64, 66
*Tradition and Education: Towards a
   Vision for Our Future* 93
Treaty No. 1 105
Treaty(ies) 16, 47, 105
Treaty No. 7 48
Trickster 69, 70, 71
Trudeau, Pierre Elliott 90
Tsuu T'ina Nation 66, 72

Underhill, Ruth 42
Union of British Columbia Chiefs 91
Union of Concerned Scientists 18
United Church 115
United States 90
University degrees 80
University of Alberta 39
University of British Columbia 90
University of Calgary 130, 134
University of Saskatchewan 121, 134
Urban reserves 140, 141

Urban transitions 140
Ursulines 83, 101

Vietnam War 90
Vision(s) 15, 45, 46, 59, 145

Walking Buffalo, Chief 137
White Paper 13, 90, 91, 92, 108
Woodland Crees 86
Wuttunee, Wiliam 91, 146
Wyoming 58

Yukon Indians 98, 139